"The most beautiful thing we can experience is the mysterious. It is the source of all true art and science. He to whom the emotion is a stranger, who can no longer pause to wonder and stand wrapped in awe, is as good as dead—his eyes are closed."

Albert Einstein

The Master Theorem

A book of puzzles, intrigue, and wit

By: M

Printed in USA
ISBN 978-0-692-18982-5

Special thanks to

Shaun Salzberg

Allison Kade

James Gibbs

Stephanie M. McPherson

Published simultaneously in the United States and interstellar space

9-15-14 16-21-12-19-1-18 1 19-5-22-5-14 9-6 23-8-25 19-8-5 20-8-5 15-6 8-5 23-8-5-18-5 8-15-23

21-16 19-20-1-18 6-9-14-5 19-5-5 25-15-21 18-15-3-11 2-5-9-14-7 9-20-19 5-7-15 23-8-15 1-18-5

20-8-5-25 6-9-22-5 10-21-19-20 22-1-19-20 23-8-5-14 12-9-6-5 15-21-20 9-14 19-5-12-6 12-9-7-8-20 8-9

8-15-21-19-5 6-9-18-5 13-5 16-9 9-20 8-5-12-16 2-5 19-9-7-14-1-12 19-15 7-15-4 3-15-13-5 21-19

5-1-20 18-1-4-9-15 16-18-9-13-5 23-5 19-5-5-13-19 6-1-18 19-5-1-18-3-8 20-18-1-22-5-12 7-15 20-23-15

8-1-14-4 15-14 12-9-11-5 8-5-18-5 20-15 23-1-12-11 26-15-15 5-12-5-22-5-14 9 23-8-25 6-15-18

20-8-5-25 18-5-1-12 8-15-23 12-9-14-5 9 15-6 19-21-14 19-8-9-16 1-14 14-1-13-5 6-12-25 1-20-15-13

20-8-5-18-5 9-20 19-20-1-18 16-15-23-5-18 4-15-23-14 1-23-6-21-12 2-5-9-14-7 8-5 21-16

5-7-15 5-14-5-18-7-25 8-9 8-5-12-16 19-8-5 23-1-19-20-5 9-14 8-21-18-18-18-25 23-8-25 19-15 8-5-5-12-12-15

16-12-5-1-19-5 15-6 12-9-6-5 12-15-22-5 6-1-19-20 2-5-9-14-7 9 1-14 23-8-5-14 9-14-20-15 20-9-13-5

5-20-8-5-18 7-1-12-1-24-25 20-1-12-11 23-5 21-19 19-20-1-18 8-5 2-21-9-12-4 19-16-1-3-5 6-1-18

Contents

How It All Began

A tap on the door in the deep of night.

A wax-sealed envelope slipped underneath.

A rustle inside and my quick escape.
Detection avoided again—but just barely.

I'm M, or at least that's how I'm known, and I'll be your guide.

I founded The Master Theorem long ago, as a secret society at my beloved alma mater. With cryptic invitations slipped under the doors of my first recruits, I wanted to do the same things that every mystery-shrouded founder of a secret society wants to do: cultivate bright young minds, spark forward-thinking debate, take over the world—you know. Think Dead Poets Society led by a Connery-era Bond.

At its core, The Master Theorem creates solvers. Our members from across the globe tackle the mysteries of the universe with their wits and wiles. They study the problems of the world and seek to make them right. They invent the ground-breaking technologies that drive our society forward. Occasionally they get distracted and build pumpkin-slinging catapults. But for the most part, they're focused on solving some of the biggest challenges known to humankind.

It was always our intention to operate in the shadows, but now more than ever the world is in dire need of solvers—and my impeccable leadership of course.

I'm therefore expanding my search for those who have the motivation—and the ability—to change the world. The Master Theorem remains a members-only society, but consider this book the cryptic invitation slipped under *your* door.

The Herculean test of your grit is as follows: Find the word or phrase solution to each one of my puzzles, called Theorems. Doing so will earn you entry into our elite ranks. It may take you some time, but trust me—it'll be worth it.

Getting Acquainted

My preferred learning style has always been: jump off cliff first, build parachute on way down. (What can I say, I'm an adrenaline junky.) But perhaps I should give you more of an orientation than that.

My puzzles, called Theorems, are not your average Sudoku or crossword puzzles. Free spirits like their creator, Theorems are more open-ended in nature, with no instructions per se. Each one is different, but solutions will always be a word or phrase.

There are 41 Theorems in this book. With somewhat of a poetic cadence to them, I recommend you solve them in order. There's no shame in skipping one or two if you get stuck, but it'll be more fun for the both of us if you go first to last.

I get that you're new at this, so I've given you three hints per Theorem. They start on page 102. Use them at your own discretion, but like Double Stuf Oreos, stay away from them unless you really need them. If you find yourself licking your lips, start with Hint #1 since it gives away the least. Move on to Hint #2 only as needed. Hint #3 won't leave much to the imagination, so if you're still stuck after that...well, we can no longer be friends.

Just kidding; you're alright.

By the way, all of my hints are encoded with a simple shift so you don't see something you don't want to while flipping through. To decode, just move each letter one place to the right. A becomes B, B becomes C, Z becomes A...you get the idea. If you need a hint to decode the hints, you may cause the universe to explode.

All that shifting can wear on your brain and you need those little grey cells for more important things. Like developing warp drive or playing Super Smash Brothers. So if you find yourself singing the BCD's more often than not, take a look at the sanity-saving thing I made for you at **http://themastertheorem.com/hints**. (Hint: It's neat.)

Full solutions for each Theorem can also be found in the back of this book, starting on page 122. But be careful, young Padawan; these are like Mega Stuf Oreos. A few words of advice:

Don't get ahead of yourself. It's possible that you may think you have the right solution to a Theorem, but are still one or two steps away. To avoid any unwelcome spoilers, I recommend that you always first check to see if your answer is right at **http://themastertheorem.com/solutions**. If it gives you the green light, then by all means, indulge in reading the full solution. If you can't check your solution online because you only have spotty internet access as you're traveling through Siberia on a secret mission (that happens to other people, too, right?), at least decode all three hints first to make sure you're on the right track.

Each Theorem will also indicate which page its solution is on. I recommend getting there by tightly flipping through the corners of the pages to find the right page number before fully opening the book. Solutions aren't encoded like my hints, so don't chance seeing something you'll wish you hadn't (though that always makes for an exciting holiday).

One more thing: I know this may be hard for you because you're in such awe of this book, but don't treat it like it's so precious. I strongly encourage you to write on and mark up these pages as much as needed to solve my Theorems and decode my hints. Your mind is the most precious thing anyway.

Alright, enough mushy stuff. Let's get going, shall we?

On the next few pages you'll find some training Theorems. Try those out now so I can be sure you've got the hang of things. Then, it's off to the races.

Training Theorems

"Education is the kindling of a flame, not the filling of a vessel."

Socrates

Practice Makes Perfect

Getting the hang of something new, like solving these Theorems, is all about starting at the basics. Think back to your nose-picking days in elementary school. In a lot of ways, becoming a master puzzle solver is like learning the alphabet and how to count—you just need practice.

And sometimes, it really can be as simple as ABC 123.

This is today,
M

TIP

First, **always read what I write** to go along with each puzzle, called a Theorem. It's not just empty words; it'll have subtle clues to help you figure out what to do.

TIP

Then, look at the puzzle itself. **It will always lead to a word or phrase answer** through some process. Go ahead and give it a try. It's nothing too difficult.

Hints: 102 • **Solution:** 122

Theorem-Solving Skill #1: Converting Numbers to Letters

When in doubt, see what happens if you translate numbers to letters and vice versa, where A is 1, B is 2, Z is 26, and so on. Essentially, **think of A - Z and 1 - 26 as interchangeable**.

TIP

I often **like using red** to mean, "Hey, look here for the final answer."

5-24-3-5-12-12-5-14-20

Aa Bb Cc Dd Ee Ff Gg
1 2 3 4 5 6 7

Hh Ii Jj Kk Ll Mm Nn
8 9 10 11 12 13 14

Oo Pp Qq Rr Ss Tt
15 16 17 18 19 20

Uu Vv Ww Xx Yy Zz
21 22 23 24 25 26

TIP

Once you've figured it out, flip the page and try the next one.

Eloquent Articulation

Do you ever reminisce fondly on the days of studying for vocab tests? Reposing by the window in the glow of a pulchritudinous spring afternoon, transcribing eccentric words onto index card after index card? Getting galvanized as those nuanced meanings embed themselves into your memory? Wasn't that just the best?

I used to count the letters of each new word I learned, back in the day. I figured if it had fewer than six, I had no use for it. But I've since learned it's not the count of letters that matters—it's what you do with them that counts.

This is today,
M

TIP

Remember to **read my ramblings for clues**. But take everything with a grain of salt; sometimes I say things just because I want to.

Hints: 102 • **Solution:** 124

Indexing means **picking individual letters out of words** to spell something else. Like taking the 1st letter of this word and 3rd letter of that word and 20th letter of another word, or whatever the puzzle implies.

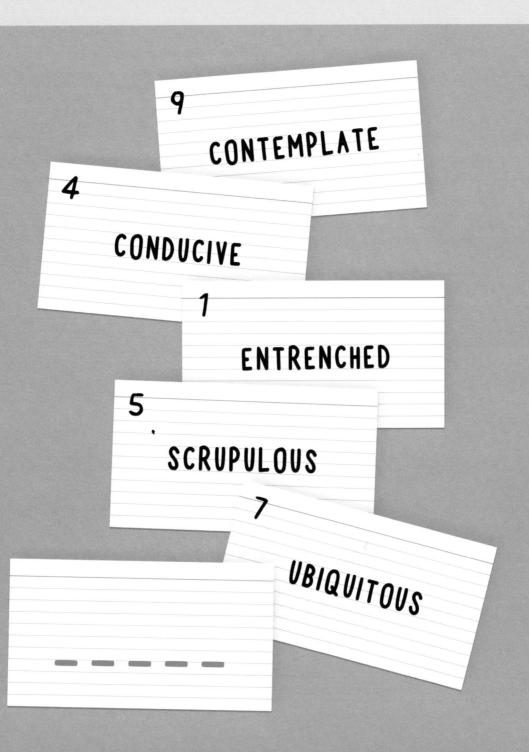

9 CONTEMPLATE

4 CONDUCIVE

1 ENTRENCHED

5. SCRUPULOUS

7 UBIQUITOUS

— — — — —

Straight to the Top

A few years ago, I was in Montenegro looking fly in a sleek tux for a casual game of poker among friends (nevermind the international stakes and the cool $10 million buy-in).

No pressure.

In these kinds of situations, I prefer not to leave my fate up to chance. So as the cards come out and the martinis kick in, I like to mentally file away what's already been played. The trick to keeping it all in your head is putting the cards in numerical order and grouping them by suit. That way you can get a pretty good sense of what might be coming next in the deck.

I wouldn't call it card counting per se—it's more like, being aware of your surroundings.

This is today,
M

TIP
It's hard to imagine I've been stumping you so far, but **try decoding the hints on this page** anyway. You may not need 'em now, but you certainly will later.

TIP
Solved it already? Then feel free to **read the full solution on this page**. Even if you don't think you need it, you might still learn a thing or two.

Hints: 102 • **Solution:** 126

What's Your Sign?

Most people wouldn't pin me as the kind of person who believes in astrology. But even I have those weeks when my computer goes on the fritz, my emails come out more sternly worded than I meant, and my long-planned NASA press conference gets cancelled at the last minute. What else am I supposed to do but blame Mercury in retrograde?

Times like those I pick up a few periodicals at the grocery store and check out my horoscope to see what the stars of the zodiac have in store for me, just in case.

This is today,
M

TIP
Don't treat this book like it's so precious. Feel free to write on these pages as much as needed to solve my Theorems.

Hints: 103 • **Solution:** 128

Theorem-Solving Skill #4: Using the Internet

Look, I know you don't know everything. So if you see something obscure, **it's okay to Google it**. It may even be required at times, so just imagine it's like I'm sending you on your own personal, digital scavenger hunt.

♊ _ _ _ _ _ _

♉ _ _ _ _ _ _

♈ _ _ _ _ _

♌ _ _

♒ _ _ _ _ _ _ _

♑ _ _ _ _ _ _ _ _ _

♎ _ _ _ _ _

♐ _ _ _ _ _ _ _ _ _ _

♓ _ _ _ _ _ _

Beware the Ides of March

Friends, Romans, puzzlers, lend me your ears! I come to warn you that puzzling can be...well... puzzling, sometimes. Especially when you get nothing more than a nonsense jumble of letters to work with.

So think of yourself like the great Julius Caesar and quash those nonsense letters like he quashed his enemies.

Just try not to turn into a dictator and get yourself assassinated.

This is today,
M

TIP
If you haven't used a hint yet, you may actually need one now. But if all that hint-decoding is wearing on your brain, check out the auto-decoder I made for you at **http://themastertheorem.com/hints**

TIP
Before you accidentally see any unwelcome spoilers in the full solution, remember that you can first check if your answer is right or not at **http://themastertheorem.com/solutions**

Hints: 103 • **Solution:** 130

Theorem-Solving Skill #5: Decoding Ciphers

Familiarize yourself with common types of ciphers—methods of encoding—that have been used throughout time. **Be on the lookout for visual and textual clues that may hint at a particular cipher**, and again, don't be hesitant to use the internet as a resource.

"ZIRM, ZMHM, ZMGM"

-CAESAR, IV

Theorems

"Science cannot solve the ultimate mystery of nature. And that is because [...] we ourselves are a part of the mystery that we are trying to solve."

Max Planck

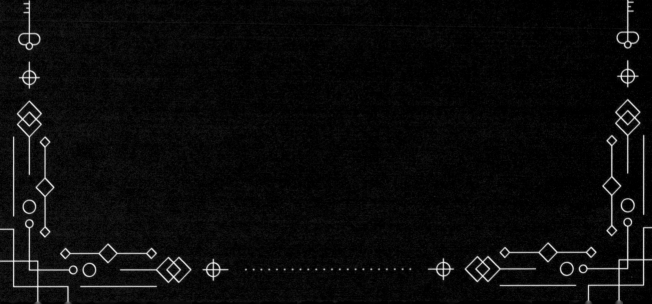

The Master Theorem

February 6

I am here.

With these words, the story of The Master Theorem officially begins. I am here, writing this book. And you are over there in your reclining chair, or airplane seat, or Hyperloop pod, reading it.

With this book we're bridging time and space to get you started on a storied journey as well. Once upon a time, you were just some average, everyday person. You had no idea what your future held. And then you saw this book. Pretty good score, if I do say so myself.

It is a truth universally acknowledged that when a story starts with an epic opening line, you know you'll be in for daring and adventure, romance and mystery. Solve all the Theorems in this book and you'll know a bit more about that firsthand.

This is today,
M

Hints: 103 • **Solution:** 132

"Sing, goddess,
Achilles' rage"

The _____

"You don't know
about me without you
have read a book by the
name of The Adventures
of Tom Sawyer"

The _____

__ _____

_____

"Call me Ishmael."

___ ____ ____

"Who's there?"

___ ____

"Emma Woodhouse,
handsome, clever,
and rich"

_____

"The story so far:
In the beginning the
Universe was created.
This has made a lot of people
very angry and been widely
regarded as a bad move."

The _____

___ ___ ____ ____

____ _____

"I've watched through
his eyes, I've listened
through his ears, and I
tell you he's the one."

____ ____

" __ ___ __ "

Masters of Many Theorems

August 18

I decided on the name "The Master Theorem" for this society because I'm inspired by the concept of what a theorem is: A truism that describes the world in a fundamental way.

I'm also borderline obsessed with the search for a "grand unified theory" that explains our universe in just a few simple equations. Which is why I didn't settle for just any theorem. Our name evokes the excitement of finally finding that "master" equation that completes the life work of Einstein and Hawking, reconciles gravity with quantum mechanics, and justifies our entire existence.

Well that, and, you know, "The Master Theorem" just sounds cool.

Theorems run the gamut from the deliciously-named ham sandwich theorem of advanced measure theory to the more useful Pythagorean theorem that every middle school kid has to memorize. Whether you learned them in grade school or grad school, theorems are guideposts for solving problems we've never seen before, and interpreting tried-and-true techniques in a novel way. The perfect steering philosophy for a society of puzzle solvers.

This is today,
M

Hints: 104 • **Solution:** 134

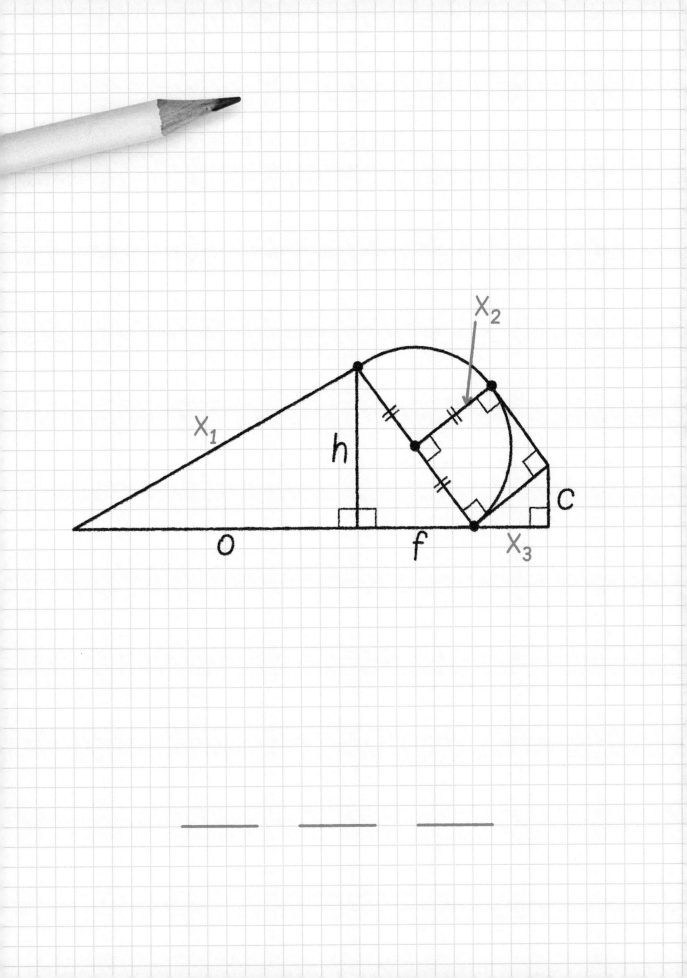

Eminent Ms

March 13

I refer to myself simply as M in order to protect my anonymity, not because I'm trying put on airs or whip out some crazy trademark like the Prince symbol on everyone. I don't want my history from before I founded The Master Theorem to interfere with this society, and I'm confident that word of mouth will spread in certain circles without involving the horde of media attention.

People ask me all the time why I chose the letter M. Could be that I'm just a big fan of McDonald's. Could be my age according to the Romans. Or it could be that I have a great deal of respect for the important Ms who came before me, many of whom were eminent figures in society, art, science, and even mythology.

As for the shifty impostors, well, I leave it up to you to weed them out.

This is today,
M

Hints: 104 • **Solution:** 136

MADISON	MINERVA	MOKO ONO
MICHELANGELO	MARX	MCCARTNEY
MADONNA	MOSES	MARCUS AURELIUS
MOLTAIRE	MIDAS	MICKEY MANTLE
MEDUSA	MANDELA	MAN BUREN
MAHLER	MAGELLAN	MERLIN
MEPPELIN	MISENHOWER	MATISSE
MORSE	MILGAMESH	MELVILLE
MENDEL	MARILYN MONROE	MALILEO
MARK TWAIN	MOSTRADAMUS	MEDEA
MARATHUSTRA	MAIMONIDES	MINCOLN
MEPHISTOPHELES	MONTAIGNE	MACBETH
MUSSORGSKY	MACHIAVELLI	MORIARTY
MALCOLM X	MOZART	MATTHEW
MOHAMMED	MONET	MAX PLANCK
MARIE CURIE	MARY	MONTEZUMA
MEETHOVEN	MICHAEL JORDAN	MACARTHUR

Different

September 28

I'm no psychic, but my money says that you're a little bit different from most people, and not in the "everyone's unique and the world is sunshine" way.

But different is good. That's how we got the theory of natural selection. And smartphones. And turduckens. It takes a certain breed of person to solve puzzles and be willing to ask some of the harder, more important questions about the world than the average Joe.

So, I commend you: Everyone else looks and acts the same, but you're a wrench. You don't rebel for the sake of being a smart aleck, but you're not afraid to stick out from the undifferentiated masses when you have something to say.

This is today,
M

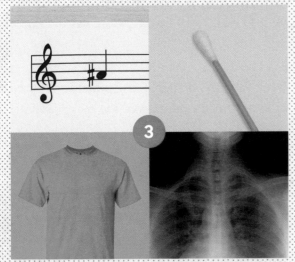

What Hath God Wrought?

April 27

Like the opening lines of literature, the first messages sent over new communication technologies tend to have a lasting impact. Just imagine if Alexander Graham Bell's first words over the telephone were, "Players gonna play play play play play, and the haters gonna hate hate hate hate hate." Okay, that would have been awesome, but to the best of my knowledge, Bell wasn't in need of shaking it off.

Some first words are simply practical: All Bell actually said was, "Mr. Watson—come here—I want to see you."

Others are comically unintentional: The first word sent over the ARPANET, the precursor of the internet, was "lo!" They were aiming for "login," but the system crashed before the message was transmitted.

But technologies that allow us to instantly talk to the other side of the world are nothing short of miracles, so my favorite first words have always been those with a little more gravitas to them. You know, something thoughtful and self-aware, with a deeper meaning than meets the eye.

This is today,

M

Hints: 105 • **Solution:** 140

L.M. Entarrie

February 8

"It is the function of science to discover the existence of a general reign of order in nature and to find the causes governing this order."

Science is kind of like the show *Law & Order*. The way I figure, scientists are simultaneously police and district attorneys. Except they don't have badges. Or guns. Though something tells me that Marie Curie with a gun would be off the hook. Maybe that should be the next spin off—*Law & Order: Radioactive Burn Unit*.

Scientists investigate phenomena, seek answers, search for truth, and use what they discover to create laws describing the universe. Newton couldn't stop at explaining why that one apple dropped to the ground. Instead, he created a whole set of laws to explain how forces govern all the movements of the world. It gives me faith that the universe is more than just mushy chaos.

Science is all about gathering relatively small data points and drawing larger conclusions. You must examine things closely and look beneath the surface—read the whole story, if you will—to understand the grander, underlying scheme.

This is today,
M

Hints: 105 • **Solution:** 142

SETTING: CRIME SCENE IN THE L.M. ENTARRIE DISTRICT, A GRID-LIKE LAYOUT OF SQUARE CITY BLOCKS. OFFICERS HYDE AND BARRY INVESTIGATING THE MURDER OF A 37-YEAR-OLD WOMAN NAMED RUBY.

(A SINGLE BEAD OF SWEAT RUNS DOWN OFFICER HYDE'S FACE.)

HYDE (FLOATING AWAY IN THOUGHT): IT'S CRAZY, YOU KNOW, SHE LIVED RIGHT DOWN THE BLOCK FROM ME, AND JUST AROUND THE CORNER FROM YOU, TOO.

BARRY: SHE WAS FROM OUR SIDE OF TOWN? WHAT WAS SHE DOING ALL THE WAY OVER HERE?

HYDE: REPORT SAYS SHE WAS CHECKING UP ON HER FRIEND, SELENE, WHO'S BEEN HAVING SOME HEALTH ISSUES. APPARENTLY SELENE IS 34, ONLY THREE YEARS YOUNGER THAN RUBY, BUT WEIGHS JUST UNDER 80 POUNDS. RUBY WAS FOUND JUST OUTSIDE OF SELENE'S HOUSE.

BARRY: WELL THEN, WE SHOULD INTERVIEW SELENE TO FIND OUT IF SHE SAW ANYTHING. YOU KNOW, I CAN'T BELIEVE THIS HAPPENED SO CLOSE TO HIS MAJESTY'S PALACE. *He* DEFINITELY WON'T BE HAPPY TO HEAR OF SUCH A CRIME IN HIS NEIGHBORHOOD.

HYDE: TRUE. LET'S NOT TELL HIM UNTIL WE SOLVE THIS CASE, THEN. FROM THE LOOKS OF IT, THIS IS THE WORK OF A GANG MARKING ITS TERRITORY. LOOKS LIKE THERE WERE FIVE, POSSIBLY SIX, SHOOTERS INVOLVED — CRAZY TO THINK THAT THE NOBLEMEN LIVE RIGHT BY THESE HOOLIGANS, TOO.

BARRY: WHICH WAY WAS THE GANG HEADED WHEN SHE WAS SHOT?

HYDE: JUDGING BY THESE TIRE MARKS, THEY HEADED SOUTH ON ROUTE 17 AT A WILD SPEED. THEY STARTED AT EXIT 9, LIKELY THE NORTHERNMOST PART OF THEIR TERRITORY, THEN ENCOUNTERED AND KILLED RUBY AT AROUND EXIT 35, RIGHT BY SELENE'S PLACE. FROM THERE, IT SEEMS AS THOUGH THEY GOT AS FAR SOUTH AS EXIT 85, WHICH MUST BE WHERE THEIR TERRITORY ENDS.

HYDE: THESE ARE DEFINITELY SOME SERIOUSLY UNSTABLE INDIVIDUALS. IT'S HARD TO BELIEVE THAT COMPLETE HUMAN BEINGS COULD DO SOMETHING LIKE THIS.

BARRY: YEAH, THIS WHOLE STREET HAS A VERY NEGATIVE VIBE TO IT. ACTUALLY, THOUGH, EVERYTHING IS STARTING TO COME TOGETHER FOR ME. I THINK I KNOW WHO THESE THUGS ARE.

HYDE: REALLY? TELL ME, *WHICH GANG* IS RESPONSIBLE FOR THIS?

Effin' Web Services

December 9

Even the mighty lose their temper sometimes.

As you may know, I've been painstakingly pulling together The Master Theorem's website with the help of my tech guy, P, and some input from my right-hand gal N. It's a neat online space where you can decode hints, check solutions, record your puzzling progress, and meet others like yourself—those brave souls who have willingly put themselves through the merriment and occasional madness of working on my Theorems. Check it out for yourself at **http://themastertheorem.com**.

But a few weeks ago, it all came crashing down thanks to an outage on the part of Amazon Web Services, or AWS. Many websites nowadays are built on top of virtual hosting services like AWS because doing so is easier than owning physical servers and hiring a dedicated system administrator.

So, long story short: when Amazon has an outage, the TMT website (along with half the internet) goes "poof." Don't get me wrong: AWS has been a godsend. But when most of the digital world relies on you, well, with great power comes great responsibility.

Luckily, we're in the clear now, but the whole incident evoked quite a strong response from P. He's usually pretty level-headed, but spending so much time in front of the keyboard could drive anyone batty.

This is today,
M

Hints: 105 • **Solution:** 144

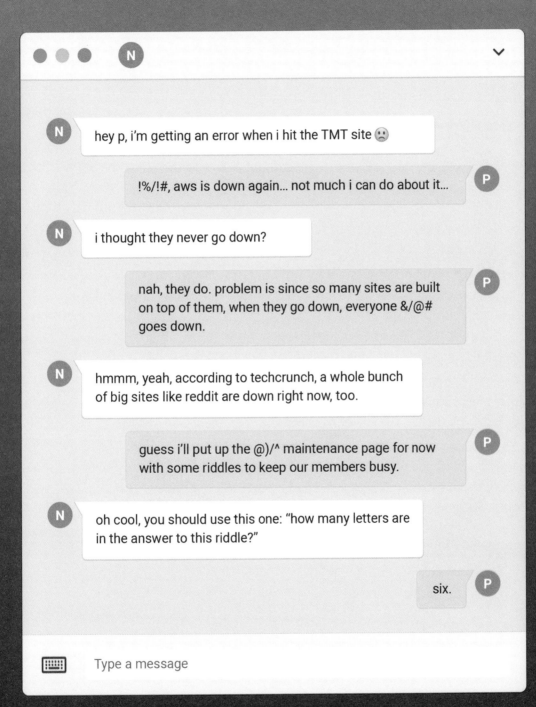

Written in the Starch

March 14

Einstein and I have much in common.

It's not just that we both have a history of unraveling the greatest mysteries of the universe. Or that we each have an excellent head of hair.

We both believe that science and spirituality can come together in one cosmic religion.

Einstein gazed at the grandeur of the stars dotting the night sky and became overwhelmed with a wonder and awe that he likened to a religious feeling. Me—I'm more partial to the Pastafarian approach.

Pastafarians follow the Church of the Flying Spaghetti Monster—or FSM, to those in the know. According to my favorite satirical religion, the FSM created the universe and has had his noodly appendage in happenings throughout human history.

While some may scoff at the idea of a carb-loaded meatball monster influencing the motions of celestial bodies, I've found proof in this starchy constellation. I've codenamed the stars appropriately. All you have to do is look at the night sky, and if you follow my reasoning, I'm sure you'll arrive at the same conclusion.

This is today,

M

Hints: 106 • **Solution:** 146

CODENAME: **PASTA**
TYPE: **SUPERNOVA**
AGE: **1 BILLION YEARS**
DISTANCE: **1 X 10^{10} LIGHT YEARS**
TEMPERATURE: **20000 K**
COLOR: **PINK**

CODENAME: **WATER**
TYPE: **TAURUS**
AGE: **1 BILLION YEARS**
DISTANCE: **18 X 10^{10} LIGHT YEARS**
TEMPERATURE: **5000 K**
COLOR: **WHITE**

CODENAME: **PENNE**
TYPE: **NEUTRON STAR**
AGE: **5 BILLION YEARS**
DISTANCE: **5 X 10^{10} LIGHT YEARS**
TEMPERATURE: **14000 K**
COLOR: **PURPLE**

CODENAME: **SAUCE**
TYPE: **URSAE MAJORIS**
AGE: **1 BILLION YEARS**
DISTANCE: **5 X 10^{10} LIGHT YEARS**
TEMPERATURE: **3000 K**
COLOR: **SUNNY**

CODENAME: ▮▮▮▮▮
TYPE: **MAIN SEQUENCE**
AGE: **1 BILLION YEARS**
DISTANCE: **14 X 10^{10} LIGHT YEARS**
TEMPERATURE: **5000 K**
COLOR: **RED**

Old McDonald

November 25

Back when I was just a wee lad working on my first Ph.D., I took a sabbatical out in rural northern Ireland. I wanted to see the stars unclouded by city lights, learn the ways of the land, and get my hands dirty.

I hadn't counted on the pigs.

I stayed on a farm owned by an eccentric old man—for a dose of poetic license, let's call him Old McDonald. He was a fun old guy, full of idioms and idiosyncrasies, and he was crazy for his pigs. He'd warn me against buying a pig in a poke, advised me to go whole hog for my dreams, and said he'd quit farming when pigs fly.

I learned a lot from that old guy and his beloved pigs. He spent more time by the pig pen than anywhere else. Which is why I was a little surprised at his seemingly haphazard pen construction: Some were missing certain walls or had round troughs in the middle. But when I stumbled upon his cryptic blueprints, I finally got the joke.

This is today,

M

Hints: 106 • **Solution:** 148

NW : N, W, S, C
NE : N, W
SW : N, W, S, E, C
SE : W, S, E, C

Move to the Beat

May 7

From Tchaikovsky to Taylor Swift—humans have a thing for music. Some, like me, also have a thing for puzzles and codes. When those two overlap, it's as undeniably enjoyable as the Beatles-meet-the-Da Vinci Code.

In 2009, a Scottish wood carver discovered a Renaissance-era wood panel engraved with a code that turned out to be musical notation. Experts believe musicians would improvise on the basic tune encoded on the panel while performing for the royal family.

It doesn't stop there. Scholars discovered that Plato seemed to use a special musical scale to encrypt his radical ideas on math and the nature of the universe within some of his other writings. (Sadly a necessity at the time, after the persecution of his homeboy and my personal hero, Socrates.)

Sometimes it goes in the other direction. Part of why I'm so intrigued by encoding puzzles in strains of music is that I like the overlap between music and math. Numbers are everywhere in music, down to the differences between quarter notes, half notes, and whole notes. This tradition has been around for a long time—famous composers like Machaut and Bach have been known to offer up puzzles in their music, leaving it to the ensemble to figure out how the piece should be performed.

For my part, I figure: Music is its own language, so why not literally make it say something?

This is today,
M

Hints: 106 • **Solution:** 150

What Some People Call Fate

October 12

Have you ever found yourself at one particular instant of time in one particular place and thought about the astronomical chances that brought you there, as you were, at that time?

That's true from the small (if I'd walked down the other side of that street last week, maybe I'd have eaten Chinese instead of pizza) to the large (if, back in college, my professor had never recruited me for the covert government project that changed my life).

If I'd never been assigned to third period gym in junior high, I might not have met my childhood best friend. And if his dad weren't a world-renowned astrophysicist, then I might never have been exposed to science the way I was. (I used to think my destiny was as a poet.)

As a result, I might have never been inspired to take that college class on quantum computing where I met my professor, and if, one day mid-college, I hadn't been loitering outside an art history class to impress a girl, I might not have chatted with that professor as he walked by. If he hadn't then mentioned his recent return from China, it might not have come up that I already knew three languages. What are the odds?

For his part, what were the chances that he'd find a kid who was great at physics (not to toot my own horn) and had the foreign language ability to help with his particular need for tech reconnaissance?

If anything had been different, I might not be here today. It's almost like every choice we make, every freak chance, spawns a parallel reality, a fully different future, even if they have a lot in common.

But I guess that's how life is, a series of chances. Better make the most of them.

This is today,
M

Hints: 107 • **Solution:** 152

Turing Test

August 29

More and more, I've been thinking about the singularity. This is the idea that artificial intelligence will be able to improve upon itself at such a rapid pace that it'll evolve well past any human intelligence and eventually make us all swear oaths to them as overlords. Okay so that last point might be paranoia fed by reading too many Elon Musk tweets. But having to deal with some sort of singularity is a very real possibility for our future.

One eerie way to think about machines taking on human intelligences is to run a Turing Test, which was designed by computer science pioneer Alan Turing in 1950 to determine a machine's ability to exhibit intelligent behavior.

Here's how it works: there's a human interrogator in one room and two subjects in another room, one human and one computer. They all communicate via text so sound of voice doesn't interfere. The interrogator asks questions and the subjects respond—the interrogator's goal is to use those responses to decide which is a human and which is a computer. If the interrogator can't figure it out, the computer passes the test and is said to exhibit intelligent behavior.

At right, you'll find a slightly modified version of the Turing Test that I've made for you. There's one interrogator and ten subjects, six of whom are human and four of whom are computers. Thing is, computer guy though I am, I've never fully trusted computers. So in this example, I know for a fact that humans always tell the truth and computers always lie.

Maybe if you interrogate the humans who have had close enough dealings with the AI, they'll let you know exactly what form the singularity will take. Then we'll know when we need to go off the grid. It's worth a shot.

This is today,
M

Hints: 107 • **Solution:** 154

INTERROGATOR >> K, SO, LIKE, WHICH OF Y'ALL R HUMANS?

SUBJECT #1 ("MAXIMILIAN") << FRANCISQUI IS A HUMAN.

SUBJECT #2 ("BERNADETTE") << I'M A HUMAN, BUT ALEKZANDER AND GEORGIANNA ARE COMPUTERS.

SUBJECT #3 ("WASHINGTON") << I'M NOT A COMPUTER, AND NEITHER IS SHIRLYANNE.

SUBJECT #4 ("ALEKZANDER") << GEORGIANNA, CRISTOPHER, AND MONTSERRAT ARE NOT COMPUTERS.

SUBJECT #5 ("MARGARETTE") << FRANCISQUI AND I ARE HUMANS.

SUBJECT #6 ("SHIRLYANNE") << MARGARETTE IS A COMPUTER.

SUBJECT #7 ("FRANCISQUI") << I'M NOT A COMPUTER.

SUBJECT #8 ("GEORGIANNA") << I'M A HUMAN, BUT MAXIMILIAN IS A COMPUTER.

SUBJECT #9 ("CRISTOPHER") << MONTSERRAT AND I ARE HUMANS, BUT BERNADETTE IS A COMPUTER.

SUBJECT #10 ("MONTSERRAT") << I'M NOT A COMPUTER, BUT FRANCISQUI IS.

Quantum Duplicity

November 22

You might not be surprised, but I have the (bad?) habit of turning the majority of my conversations to the topic of quantum mechanics.

You say: "Aren't you glad that the weather is finally warming up?"

I reply: "Aren't you glad that the Large Hadron Collider can smash high energy proton beams together at near light speed, revealing a shower of subatomic particles the likes of which have never been observed before?"

Actually, these topics aren't as different as you might think. Whether you're talking about the weather or quantum mechanics, you're talking about the fundamentally probabilistic nature of our universe. We can't say with any surety where a given particle is at any given time, only where it is most likely to be. Just like you can't be any more precise than "there's a 50 percent chance of rain a week from Wednesday."

But here's my favorite part, where quantum mechanics gets way cooler than the weather: the reason you can't know the location of a particle before observing it is because certain subatomic particles can actually exist in two places at once. Seriously. The same identical particle, two locations, same time. It's like a B-level sci-fi flick.

Which raises all sorts of questions that are way more interesting than the weather. My cat Schrödinger agrees.

This is today,
M

GAUGE

PHOTON

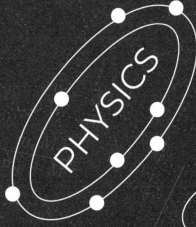
PHYSICS

PROBABLE

HEIGHT

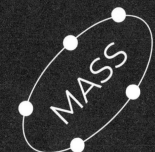
MASS

FEYNMAN

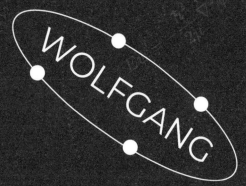
WOLFGANG

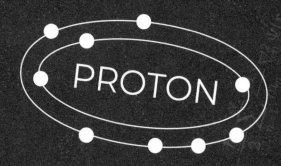
PROTON

FERMIONIC

8-Bit Classics

I was rummaging through my attic last weekend for my copy of the collected works of Cicero, when I stumbled across my old Nintendo. I put down the ancient Roman philosophy, picked up the ancient early 90s technology, and thought, "Man, I loved those 8-bit classics!"

Duck Hunt, Zelda, Punch-Out!!—each is a symphony of 0s and 1s racing through a little gray box to produce images as evocative as Botticelli's *Venus*. Well, kind of. I remember spending hours racing my Excitebike past blurred shrubbery, hunting computerized ducks, and running from crazy-eyed ghosts.

For me, it's less about each specific game than the fact that game design as a whole was much simpler back then. Without the 3D graphics and orchestral music production of today's multi-million dollar video games, these 8-bit ancestors created simple, engaging worlds with clear binary distinctions between up and down, on and off, here and there, good and evil. Gamers like me appreciated the beauty of these simple worlds in which every little bush, platform, and coin had a purpose.

This is today,
M

Hints: 108 • **Solution:** 158

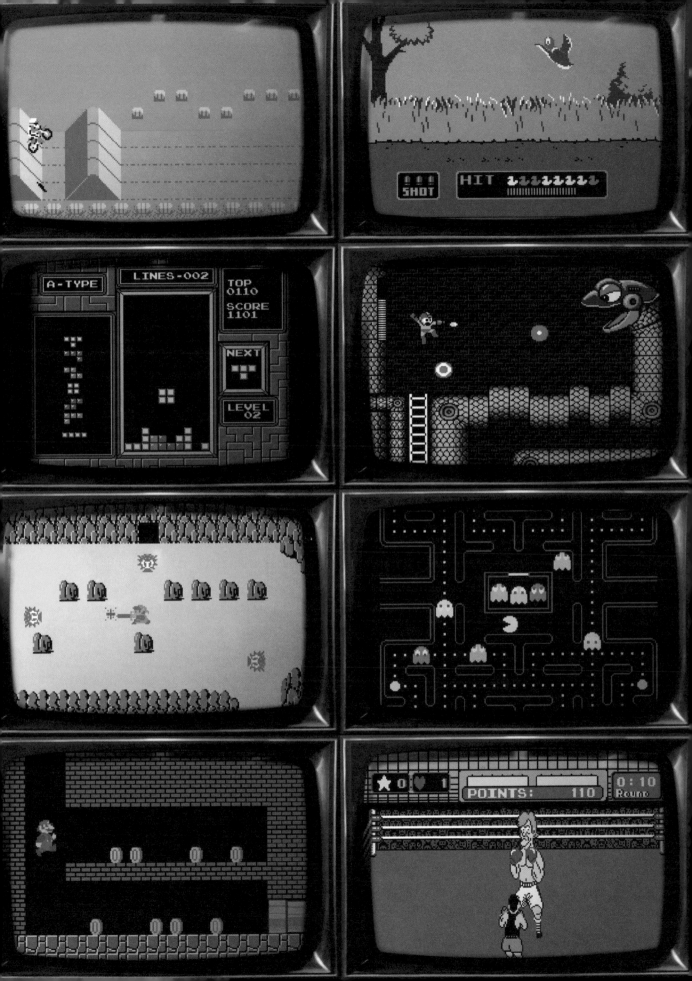

The Final Revelation

July 1

Egocentric beings that we are, at every point in human history we've thought ourselves to be at the center of everything. But each time, without fail, we've been wrong.

Since the horizon seems equally far away in all directions, thousands of years ago we naively concluded that Earth was a flat round disc and we were at its center. But as most of us now know (excepting an odd flat-Earther or two on Twitter), our planet is, in fact, a sphere, and therefore with no center.

That clearly didn't stop us from thinking we were special, though, with a central place in the universe. *Okay*, we thought, circa the 15th century. *Maybe we're not at the center of the earth, but the earth is the center of the solar system, right?* Nope. *Oh, so everything revolves around the sun? Okay, well at least our solar system is at the center of the galaxy, right?* Wrong again. *But our galaxy is for sure at the center of the universe? And our universe is the only one out there?* No and (probably) no!

Nowadays, we of course know that the Milky Way is just a single, unremarkable galaxy in a vast universe filled with a hundred billion other galaxies, that the universe is expanding in such a way that there is no "center," and that even the whole universe may just be one of an infinite number of universes in a twisted version of reality called the multiverse.

So, over the years, we humans have clearly had many eye-opening, decentralizing revelations about our place in the universe. But that makes me wonder: what's next? What's that final revelation? What thing—like ourselves, the earth, the galaxy, and the universe—do we still consider to be so important as to be at the center of everything? But may one day be shown to not be as central to the world as we think?

Please don't tell me it's Oreos.

This is today,
M

Hints: 108 • **Solution:** 160

Sleep is the Station Grand

December 10

Today, I bring you something I know you've been craving since day one: a front-row seat in the observation deck of my mind. Recently, I've started keeping track of all the weird stuff my brain does in an attempt to document its inner workings. Here, I give you a glimpse at what my mind does in those fuzzy moments right before I drift off to sleep.

And if you think I'm strange when I'm awake, you should really meet my half-asleep alter ego.

In my almost-unconscious state, I hear a myriad of voices that all begin to run together. Some sound like voices I know, some don't. Some are words and phrases I've heard before, some aren't. Either way, as they rapidly race through the space between my ears, they all mix and match and merge together, producing utterly nonsensical ramblings. But, hey, I'm a creative at heart.

It's so fascinating to me that I've recorded hundreds of these quirky sound bites in my bedside journal. What I love about it all is that despite this cacophony of synaptic firings in the maze of my neurons, it often ends up sounding surprisingly beautiful—almost poetic.

This is today,
M

Hints: 109 • **Solution:** 162

A NINE DOLLAR
BILL IN THE SUN

MAKE WEIGHT
EXPLOSIVES

WOH, META-LOOP, LOOP OF FIRE

LAVA BRAIN

OH, THE YELLOW PAPER?

IS...RENO...GOD?

IS THIS A FRAME?

WHO'S FACING
THEM AWAY

IT JUST CAME OUT
AT THE 8-80

FOR A PILLOW
TO PERFORM

A ROCK BURN POUND,
A PARTICLE MINT

TODAY WOULD BE A GOOD DAY FOR A NEW SUIT WAIVER

HEFT? THAT DOESN'T WORK

AND MY CHALKBONE

LOOPTIT SON,
INOTEMPT POUND

EVEN THE RARE
ENZYMES DIFFER

THEY HAVE LIKE 500% WILD
ANIMALS DOWN THERE

VERONICA WILL SHOVE ITS
TEMPLAR IN THE RAIN

IF A SANDWICH FALLS INTO IT

SIR, YOU'RE LEAKING
AS THE POLITICAL
APPROACH

LIKE THE HUBBLE
SYLLABLE

THEY DON'T HAVE A
SMALL NUMBER HERE

YO FROM THE BLUE TEAM

YOU DO NOT GIVE UP
ON YOUR P-TYPE

YOU SOUND LIKE
AN INJURED CAR

Who in the Where with the What

I don't have a ton of free time, but when I do, one of my favorite ways to spend it is to read mystery novels. My tastes aren't terribly high-brow, either—the more cliché the better. There's something about the swashbuckling detective and eccentric characters in a whodunit that makes the form a classic.

After experiencing enough Sherlock Holmes twists and watching an excessive number of *Bones* episodes, I've decided that I'm a prime candidate to become a bestselling mystery novelist. (You may have already had the pleasure of reading one of my earlier classics, L. M. Entarrie.)

At any rate, you just have to follow the basic formula, give your detective a rugged name like Gregoire or Wynter or Dyce, make him ooze sex appeal, and leave clues for your readers to try to guess the villain.

This is today,
M

Hints: 109 • **Solution:** 164

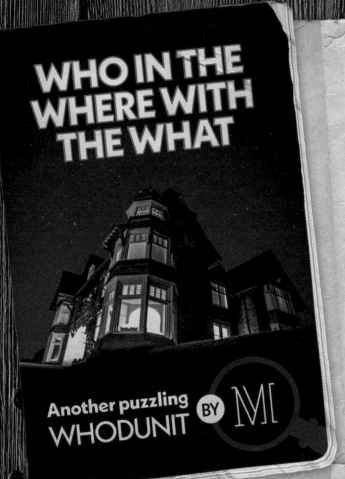

WHO IN THE WHERE WITH THE WHAT

Another puzzling **WHODUNIT** BY M

Detective Rafe Koontz, dashing as always sauntered onto the crime scene. "What have we here?"

The victim, Seymour Boddy, had been rushed to the hospital after being attacked. The perp had moved him, so police didn't have the weapon or know where he was attacked either. Of course, Rafe was the best (and sexiest) crime-solver around. He'd get to the bottom of this.

The police led Rafe past the entrance hall to the lounge, where the suspects were assembled for questioning.

Rafe flashed his dastardly grin at a sultry woman on the velvet couch. She winked. "Sweetie, it couldn't have been me. I was in the library on the phone with my dear old mother when it happened. I discovered him outside, still holding the plum that he'd been eating. Gut-wrenching to see."

Rafe nodded. "What was your relationship to Mr. Boddy?"

Her face turned scarlet. "He was a bit of a womanizer, you know. I left him after he started having an affair with the housekeeper." She pointed to a woman across the room, who was wearing a maid's white apron. "Granted, she couldn't have attacked him, either. She wasn't here on kitchen duty today." She smiled seductively. "As for me, I'm focused on stardom. I practice at the conservatory. You should swing by to see me perform in the ballroom sometime."

"Enough flirting." said the man next to her jealously. He wore an old-fashioned green vest and a top hat. "Taste in women aside, I was good friends with Boddy," he told Rafe. "We regularly smoked a pipe together in the study."

Rafe moved on to a guy wolfing down fried chicken smothered in honey mustard. "You're slobbering like this during an investigation? Where were you this afternoon?"

"Dude, sorry, I'm tired from shooting pool in the billiard room all day. Though I did hate

Seymour Boddy — he might as well have put a revolver to my head, considering how badly the investments he sold me failed."

The maid tapped Rafe on the shoulder. "Maybe it was the newest woman he roped in. He took her out for a romantic supper last week, complete with champagne and candlesticks and all that," she said bitterly.

"Maybe."

A policeman pulled Rafe aside. "The victim is in recovery at the hospital. And, sir, we found a feather inside the pocket of the suit he was wearing."

Rafe flashed his handsome smile. "The key is what's been left unsaid. I know who did it, where, and how."

Everyone cheered and the day was saved.

Geocaching

May 28

Recently I had a few hours to kill atop KwaDuma peak in Lesotho and decided to see if there were any geocaches around.

In case you haven't heard, geocaching is an international "sport" that involves finding hidden boxes (kind of like secret treasures) at particular GPS coordinates. I've got the Geocaching app on my phone, of course, and to my pleasant surprise there was a cache squirreled away near the summit on my route back to camp (where I found some traditional oxtail stew waiting for me. Food tourism: a major must of international travel).

Usually, when you find a cache—which can be anything from run-of-the-mill tupperware to more stealthy stone-shaped canisters—there's at least a logbook inside so you can leave your mark among all the other intrepid explorers who've found it as well.

But it shouldn't be surprising that a nerdy activity all about discovering hidden treasures has lots of complicated varietals. I'm particularly drawn to the virtual cache, which has you finding interesting locations rather than actual objects, and the puzzle cache, which has you solving clues until you decode the coordinates of a final location.

Puzzle caches are obviously my jam and I'm sure you're quite comfortable on your couch right now, so I've made a virtual puzzle cache for you. It's almost like you and I took a private vacation together around the globe. That'd be a dream come true, I know.

This is today,

M

Hints: 109 • **Solution:** 166

48° 51' 29.24" N, 2° 17' 40.26" E

A = The number of levels it has

37° 58' 17.35" N, 23° 43' 35.90" E

B = The total number of columns once along its outside perimeter

39° 55' 01.17" N, 116° 23' 27.65" E

C = The number of structures (gates and towers) that sit directly on the surrounding wall

33° 51' 25.64" S, 151° 12' 54.51" E

D = The total number of shell-like sections on the roofs of all three structures

40° 41' 21.01" N, 74° 2' 40.43" W

E = The number of points on the star-shaped platform

FINAL CITY	= (B+A+1)° (D÷5+A)' (E+A+2).(CxA−1)" N
	(C+D−4)° (B÷2+2)' (D−C+E).(B+D+C)" E

N70°
Arctic Circle

N50°

N30°

Shifty Financial Business

September 29

The Master Theorem—and its members—are pretty much everywhere. At some time or other, I've known members who are engineers, politicians, acclaimed artists, circus clowns, and, alas, finance people. Don't worry, I tend to attract the honest, genuinely-thinks-economics-is-fascinating types.

One such financially-inclined member recently turned to me for help. She was a young investment banker who witnessed and felt the 2008 economic crisis in the United States firsthand. Even as the recession officially came to a close, she needed to know more about what had happened and why (as The Master Theorem members are wont to do). As she investigated, she kept finding patterns in the record books that didn't make sense. Possessed by the feeling that something just wasn't right, she shared her suspicions with her trusted puzzle-solving confidantes.

"I think this might have something to do with the shifty financial practices that started the recession in the first place," she told me. In particular, she kept coming back to a very specific group of historical stock figures. She thought they might tie the financial crisis to things that continued for years after the recession began. "Can you help me figure out what's really happening here?"

Well, can you?

This is today,

M

Hints: 110 • **Solution:** 168

Ticker	Change	Date
TGI Telecom General Industries	+15.00	3/6/09
JE Jackson Electric	+1.00	10/28/08
MRW Macro Renewable Wind	-22.00	9/14/08
SXQ Six Quanta, Inc.	+10.00	5/10/11
QZC Quantum Zoom Commerce	-1.00	3/12/10

NYSE

NYSE

Of Siberia, Word Parts, and You

About a year ago, I found myself in a private train car with my colleagues N, O, and P, coasting through the oddly beautiful Siberian wilderness.

Somewhere between Irkutsk and Kamensk, P turned his pensive gaze from the lake outside the window towards us and smiled. "Can you think of a word that has BMA in it as a whole?"

SUBMARINE wasn't too hard for us to get, especially while surrounded by constant reminders of the Cold War and Soviet-era Russia. But it was certainly interesting to think that a strange letter combination like BMA could exist in English, and it spawned a fantastic word game we've been playing with each other to this very day.

It's even helped us launch The Master Theorem's gaming wing, TMT Games. Maybe you know this part of the story: our flagship word game, Snippets®, was released in 2016, and it's not-so-unintentionally similar to P's road-trip game.

What you may not know is that I initially wanted Snippets to be...well...a little more difficult. Now, "anything goes" in the game including proper nouns and slang, making it more approachable for the general public. But in the original version, only dictionary words were allowed, and I even ensured that each "snippet" only appeared in one (common) word in the entire English language.

[Insert maniacal laugh here.]

Eventually, my marketing team convinced me that the game should have a broader appeal, and legal didn't want game boxes with our logo being thrown from 12th-story apartment windows in fits of rage anyway. But early drafts of the game still exist, hidden away, waiting for a brave puzzler to attempt them.

This is today,
M

Hints: 110 • **Solution:** 170

RKB

OYR

LPF

GEV

FEG

HWH

PWR

FWA

DPE

ITP

SNI PP ETS®

ROUND

ANSWER PAD

Ancient Crosswords

Today's society on the whole may not fully appreciate the art of puzzling, but my predilection for puzzles grows out of a long tradition. Even the ancient Romans liked a good crossword puzzle: The Sator Square, first found in the remains from Pompeii, is a four-times palindrome built into itself with the words interlocking. When anagrammed in a certain way, it can be unraveled to form a cross shape with the words "Pater Noster" running both top to bottom and left to right, intersecting in the middle. There's an A and an O left over on each side of the cross, symbolizing Alpha and Omega, or the beginning and the end.

The Master Theorem is so awesome that it may feel like a religion, but the Sator Square actually held Christian connotations for the Romans, and it sometimes even took on magical and folk uses over time.

Sure, I'd also like my place in the pantheon, but I am, sadly, a mere mortal. They do say doing crosswords can keep your brain sharp, though. Maybe that will be good enough.

This is today,

M

L A D D G

A E E M O

I K O K I

O M E E A

G D D A L

RECURSIVE: ADJ. SEE RECURSIVE

September 9

Back when I was just a teenager, I did a stint as a software engineer at NASA's Jet Propulsion Laboratory. As a welcome gift, a colleague gave me one of those wooden puzzles where you have to fit a bunch of Tetris-like pieces together into a rectangular box.

Now, you know me: I love all sorts of puzzles. But not this kind. This was one of those puzzles all about brute force. No clever solutions here; you just have to try a bunch of things until it works. But it kills me to leave a puzzle unsolved, so I still spent hours fiddling with the pieces, moving them and rotating them and getting more and more frustrated because they just...wouldn't...fit.

Later that day, my colleague came into my office to ask me a question about the code we were writing for calculating Viking 2's landing coordinates. He noticed the puzzle, abandoned, on my desk, and gave me some serious flak for it

So, in a fit of youthful, indignant rage, I neglected my job for the rest of the day, and did what programmers do best: I wrote a program to solve the puzzle for me.

I was fairly proud of it: a cleverly constructed, recursive, breadth-first search algorithm (where all my programming geeks at?). For you coding muggles, a "recursive" function is one that refers to itself from within itself, using its outputs as its own inputs, which creates a loop of sorts, but one that eventually ends and helps the original function arrive at an answer. You have to be careful when designing recursive functions, though. Depending on how they're coded and their initial inputs, they may go on forever and cause some nasty out-of-memory errors.

Later that day I sauntered over to my colleague's office, dropped a massive print-out of nearly a thousand unique solutions on his desk, and walked out without a word. In TMT and in life, it's never about brute force.

This is today,
M

Hints: 111 • **Solution:** 174

```
Z  S F H J V I U K L P O U V X Z U E L V N E E W Q P K
Y  A M B M N A Q O P K J H C U Y T A Z M L P O V G A L
X  M V X U G F S P I I J G Z L F D T S W B C L K A U I
W  B F W K T G H C S I O A E B N F M N H P O F D S V M
V  A W C B O H J F I T R D M N C S L P I Y G N B M K L
U  A K N I U H M G D Y H H O T G N B D Y O K V Z X J O
T  M B T E R U I U Y J K D R E G B M W L N F O I P P
S  B W E B A E E M H B V C D W Q K L F G V U Y I Z X F
R  G N J U E F R E K L O P H G W V D S Q W O B N M J K
Q  N V Z X Y U L K J M F E U R T Y P O P O O O O M W X
P  C T G U H J K M U C D U G H T R W Q N B V C X Z M K
O  O I Y H G H E V F G G I O H Y T R R W S V F D R E E
N  M G H J K J K K O U I E S A U B M N J U T Y D F L L
M  P I U B V G N D R E Q M K G U Y T X D C B I Y M P H
L  U V N F J Y T R E E E C A D H G U J O K B V X Q A
K  A F E W E R T Y H B C B C N Z A W Q H J I U M K L K
J  M H F I G L L V Y T E Z F U K J G V U Y E T R R O P
I  M H G F C R Z I U Y H J N I I G Y F O E Q W B J K L
H  M G W C V J O H F M U T R E R R R T Y N N T M G F
G  A X F J I Y T E T N V X Z Z B H L M N M H E
F  F Z B A U I G F D J T R F C B X Z O P J H G N B E L
E  E L E Q W E G A G J U I U K L N H R I T S S P R E H K
D  D A O O O O O H B W Q B D F U I K M J U Y T G F C V L
C  C L U T F L J O M H G F H U A T R D F C V J H I U I U
B  B M J G H I U Y B F S E D I L K N B A W Q C I J N B N
A  A L F R A N U Y N G F D J M J H Y T R I U N I J K S G
   A B C D E F G H I J K L M N O P Q R S T U V W X Y Z
```

_ _ _ _ _ _ _ _ _ _ > _ _ _ _ _ _ _ _ _ > _ _ _ _ _ > _ _

Birds, Bees, and Strange Amalgams

April 22

In warm weather, one of my favorite pastimes is to relax on the breezy terrace by my private lake, ruminating. My garden is a menagerie of sorts, housing many different creatures in the ecosystems from which they come so that they'll be comfortable. While recently gazing at the carp in my lake and the colorful birds in my personal aviary, I thought about the incredible diversity of life on Earth.

Sure, there are always run-of-the-mill birds and bees, but I'm attracted to the creepy, the weird, the strange amalgams of the world. The impetus to build this home for my favorite fauna came after a series of outdoor adventuring trips. Whether I was rock climbing or scuba diving, I kept pausing to ask (or bubble underwater), "What's that one called?"

After all, in addition to the wide array of animals out there, there are also tons of ways to name those animals. (Who, for example, got to decide that a creepy, vaguely vomit-looking sea creature should be named "pancake fish"?)

Want to know my favorite creature of all time? All you have to do is take a look at some of the other creatures in my garden, figure out what they have in common, and then put them in order.

This is today,

M

Hints: 112 • **Solution:** 176

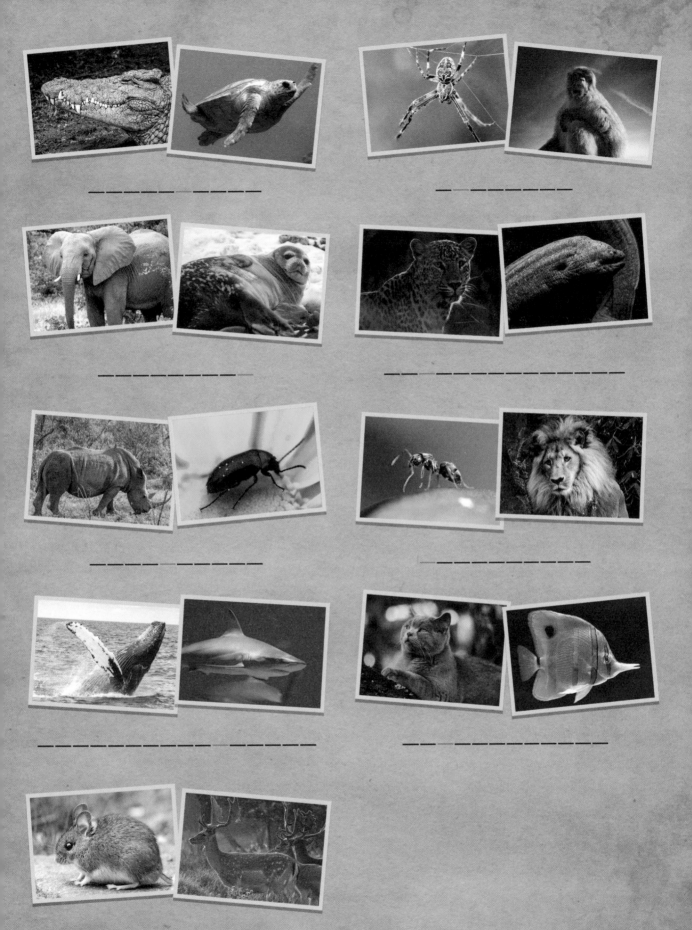

Precision Paintball

June 3

I'm of the mind that everything could be improved with a little bit more tech. (I know, I know—shocking.) This extends to my downtime, too. On weekends, I like to play paintball, but not just your grandma's paintball. When I play, it looks like a futuristic robot-wars battlefield.

See, I used to build advanced weaponry for the military before I became a pseudo-pacifist after spending some unexpected time in the deserts of Afghanistan. And while I no longer want to profit from war machines, I can't help but tinker with weapons of lesser destruction, aka paintball guns.

Not to toot my own horn, but I've been fairly prolific in my field, too. Over the years, I've built homing paintballs, proximity-detecting paint landmines, and app-controlled paint-spewing drones. I've even got autonomous robots that carry all my gear.

I'm familiar with the usual rules of paintball, like Capture the Flag and King of the Hill. But creative that I am, I often prefer to make up my own variations to the game. Lately, my cryptographer buddies that I like to paintball with have been complaining that I don't play fair, what with all my gadgets and complicated varietals. They claim that the key to paintball should simply be physical prowess.

Well. They want me to play fair? I'll play fajr. They want physical prowess? I'll show them physical prowess. I've been cooking up a new variant of paintball that will leave them with welts for weeks!

This is today,

M

Hints: 112 • **Solution:** 178

Synesthesia

January 11

I've said it before and I'll say it again: Brains are weird. From the seemingly nonsense connections of my mind in the minutes before sleep to the way I perceive numbers and letters, my mind (and your mind, I'd bet) is a mystery.

For whatever reason, I strongly associate letters and numbers with specific colors. When I look at printed text, I don't actually see the various colors—I know the text is black—but my subconscious immediately calls up the related color in my head. Sometimes that association is so strong that when I'm trying to remember some word or name, I can often recall the color of the word before the word itself.

This phenomenon, called synesthesia, is well-documented, but the actual text-color associations work differently for everyone. My associations are documented at right, and my personal synesthesia seems to follow these rules:

· Whole words appear to me as the same color as their first letter
· Multi-digit numbers are beautifully multi-colored, as determined by their individual digits

Makes the whole world just a touch more colorful, you know?

This is today,

M

Hints: 112 · **Solution:** 180

A	B	C	D	E
F	G	H	I	J
K	L	M	N	O
P	Q	R	S	T
U	V	W	X	Y
Z	1	2	3	4
5	6	7	8	9

25 BACON BITS VANILLA 29 BROWNIES AND ALLSPICE 2

Ethical Hacking

November 8

Despite my deep love for this country and my many years of dedicated service for our government, I recognize that our politicians can sometimes fail us.

Whether due to ignorance or the intentional disregard for science and data, they often make decisions and policies that are clearly bad for the country, harmful to the planet, or even suppress whole groups of people. The most important way to combat this, of course, is to be well informed and make good decisions at the ballot box.

But, between you and me, there are also...other...ways to push back when simply voting isn't enough. I spent years in the cyber warfare unit of an agency that shall remain unnamed, working to overthrow oppressive governments around the world, and I realized something profound: When you have a fluency in science, engineering, and how stuff works in general, you have a lot more power than you even realize.

In your case, say you're a whiz with electronics and you know a new, highly-guarded bill relating to the environment is about to be presented to Congress. You suspect some shady business is going on, and you need to get your environmental lobbyist friends prepared for immediate action. Now, of course, I'm not advocating that you actually do this, but you could, hypothetically-speaking, pretend to apply for an internship with a key senator, get invited for an interview, stealthily snatch a USB thumb drive from his briefcase while he's not looking, use your circuit-bending know-how to solder a few jumper wires in the right places, and the next time he plugs it into his computer, gain remote access to all his files so you can read the bill for yourself and be prepared to lobby against that dastardly deal to turn the Everglades into a golf resort.

I wouldn't call this cyber warfare necessarily, but "ethical hacking" perhaps?

This is today,
M

Hints: 113 • **Solution:** 182

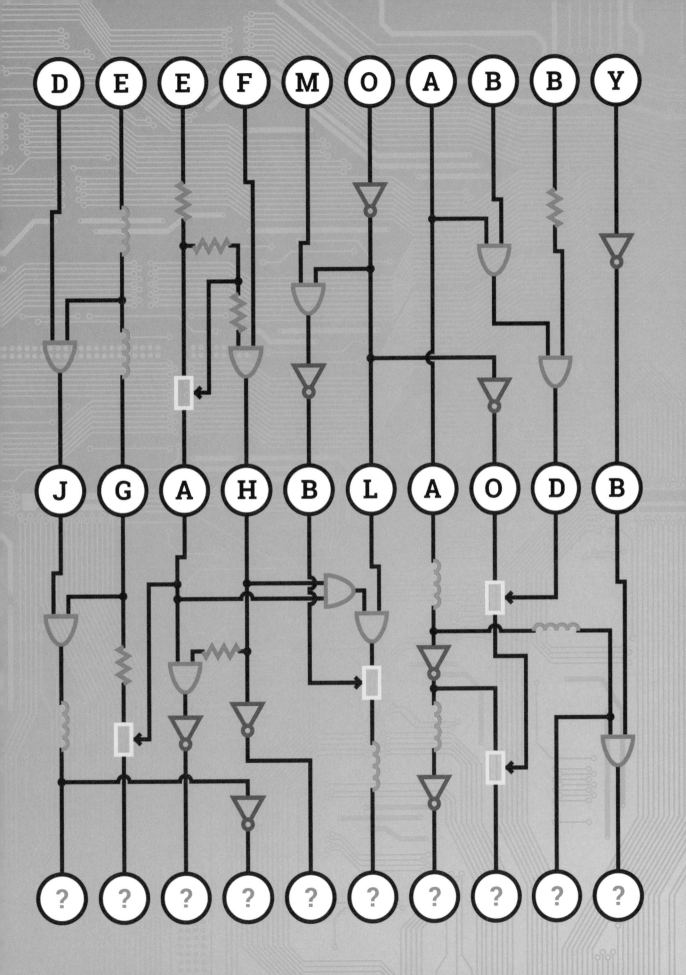

Stay Puzzly, My Friends

February 20

Remember all those commercials for Dos Equis beer? You know, the ones with the guy who's supposedly the most interesting man in the world? He pulls it off pretty well—look him up and you'll be almost taken in by his penetrating gaze and salt-and-pepper scruff.

But here's the thing that's always infuriated me: That guy's just an actor. He's never found sunken treasure or arm wrestled an army general in the jungle. Ahem.

I've heard it said that my own biography is a bit fantastical in its own right, so I'm taking this opportunity to help you get to know me better. We're going to play the game called "two truths and a lie." In each group to the right, I've written three "facts" about myself, two of which are true, and one of which is a lie. Not that anything here is a terribly far stretch for me, but can you weed out which ones are false?

Now let's see who the most interesting man in the world really is, shall we?

This is today,

M

Hints: 113 • **Solution:** 184

Smitten with language, I now speak exactly five including English, Mandarin, and Hindi.

Russia, Haiti, and South Africa are just a few of the many countries I've called home.

I've gone diving off the coast of Micronesia to explore sunken WWII ships.

I lived in Moscow for all of 1992 where I learned Russian for an upcoming assignment.

When *The Scream* was stolen, I moved to Oslo in 1994 to help police recover it.

Tired from a lengthy mission, I moved to a remote island in 1991 for four years straight.

I've been rock climbing in South America.

Every year I go BASE jumping.

I've gone wreck-diving in the Pacific.

In my free time, I like to program simulations of fluid dynamics and galaxy formations.

My entire research career was devoted to astrophysics, studying the likes of dark matter.

Long interested in stress responses, every summer I jump off skyscrapers with sensors.

I helped the government translate tense Japanese/North Korean transmissions in 2009.

Longing for an edgier pursuit, I led the team that stole Edvard Munch's *The Scream*.

Back in 2006, I was part of a team that scaled up Mount Roraima in Brazil.

All the way back in my research days, I developed a new drug to treat certain cancers.

Trained as a classical cellist, I've performed with three world-renowned orchestras.

I own a 30-foot telescope that rivals the one at the Keck Observatory.

Murder at Sea

July 12

After my blockbuster whodunits from past Theorems (you may recall a pair of elementary detectives and a winding mansion full of clues), you might start to think that M stands for Master of the Murder Mystery. How about one more to make you certain?

In this whodunit installment, we travel to the high seas. Think of movies like *Crimson Tide, The Hunt for Red October*, and *U-571*. This story is just like that. I suspect Hollywood has already flagged it for the big screen treatment.

Imagine intrigue, deception, and dramatic weather that just so happens to illustrate the intensity of the scene. If you want to be a superstar writer like me, that's all you need—a flair for drama and just a touch of finesse.

Oh, and mad skills. Hope you learn a thing or two from this masterwork.

This is today,
M

Hints: 114 • **Solution:** 186

General Stanley McDouglas looked out pensively upon the sea, listened to the sound of the ship's flag flapping in the wind, and took in the salt air. It was 9:25. But this unusual time of stillness should have been a red flag.

Around 9:35, most of the crew was playing poker in the mess hall. The Kamchatka Strait was behind them, the open ocean before. For the first time in a long time, Lt. Todd Swift was cleaning up at a game of five-card draw when the general burst in and said, "Take your stations and flag down the rest of the crew. Radar signals detect a massive storm approaching. Only time will tell how bad it will actually be."

They resumed their posts uneventfully until 7:30 that night. They'd remember that as the time when all hell broke loose. The skies suddenly opened up and the wind roared mercilessly as the ship's flag tore violently from side to side. "We've got incoming!" an officer shouted.

Then, the commotion suddenly stopped. As the skies cleared up, General McDouglas took time to make a sweep of the premises and even though parts of the ship were still submerged in waist-deep water, everything seemed fine. With reservations, he flagged down the ship's navigator to resume course.

At 9:15 a scream came from the crew's partially flooded quarters. Lt. Swift had been found dead, brutally murdered.

The general immediately flagged down the crew and signaled them to search the ship for stowaways. Maybe, the crew whispered, there's a spy on board. Or maybe, there's something else. The search lasted a long time—until about 7:00 in the morning—but found nothing.

"Walk me through this again," General McDouglas questioned his executive officer the next day. "You said that at 7:25 you saw suspicious movement on the front bow?"

"No," his right-hand man said. "It was 7:30, right around the time the storm began."

"So you followed shadowy figures around until 12:30? That didn't seem like a red flag to you?"

The engine rumbled ominously. "Yessir, it did… But as the flood waters receded off the ship, it seemed as though we were all in the clear beginning around 9:55."

"Heaven help us all. **Who, or what**, is responsible for this?"

Prison Life

Back in my Count of Monte Cristo days, I would stare at the dull brick walls in despair, knocking out my memoir on the broken down typewriter I'd found in the library of Alcatraz. Which was where I'd spend the rest of my downtrodden years.

Just kidding. But I do kind of wish I could go back to the Rock during the gangster days of Scarface in the 30s, or find out the real story behind the escape of Frank Morris and the Anglin brothers. Can't you just imagine them tapping away at those secret passages with tiny little tools? There's something very Shawshank Redemption about it all.

Definitely, life was hard. Prisoners were dangerous. And they had to survive by tapping into pretty limited resources. But that prison island has really ingrained itself in popular culture, and, I'm not gonna lie, it's embedded itself pretty deeply in my own imagination. I often relax at home in my orange pajamas, wondering what it would be like to be one of those hardened criminals with a killer nickname serving out his years.

Not that I'm not. I could have scratched out this draft on a roll of toilet paper to the sounds of my cellmate's snores.

This is today,

M

Hints: 114 • **Solution:** 188

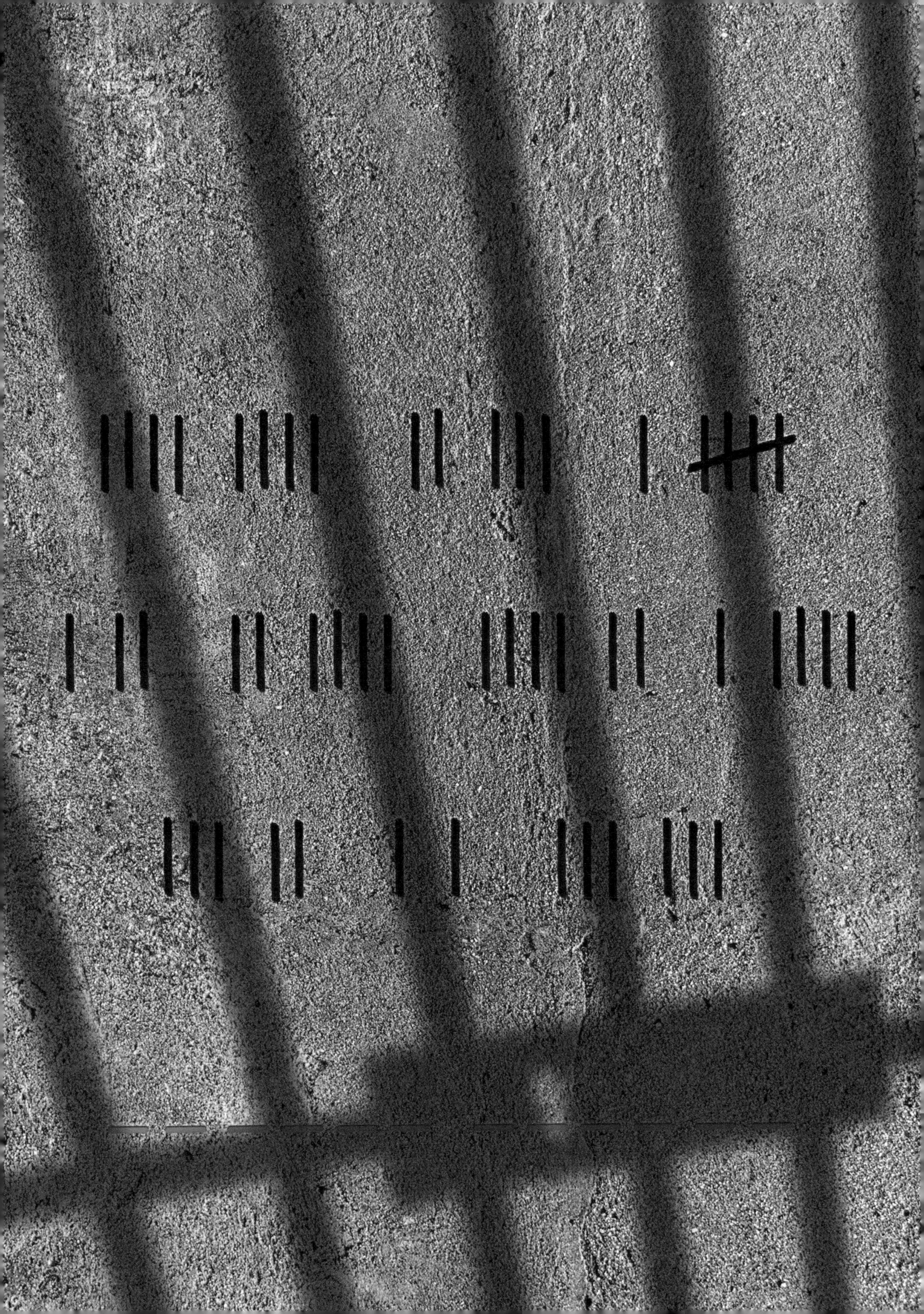

My Basement

May 5

I wouldn't feel as though I'd met my full potential in life if I hadn't realized my dream of living in an enormous puzzle house. As a kid, I used to base my self worth on how many hours I spent drawing blueprints for my eventual home. Puzzles were hidden in the furniture, moldings, tiles, and, of course, there were secret passages throughout.

Basically, when it came time for me to get my own home, I based the design on my blueprints from years before. Nowadays, it's a five-story house with puzzles on each floor, and they all interrelate. If you follow each puzzle to the next, you eventually find yourself in my favorite of the secret rooms: the basement. I spend most of my time here thinking, listening to music, and writing these Theorems that you've come to know and love.

I built one additional puzzle in that basement as a fun side project—a mural of colorful tiles based on geometric patterns. I like geometric designs because of the mathematical elegance that they're based on, and I hope you'll like my mural because, you know, I'm surprisingly artistic.

This is today,
M

Hints: 114 • **Solution:** 190

Of Math and Manischewitz

March 23

As you may have realized by now, I tend to nerd out about all things math. But my all-time favorite math-y things are prime numbers—or those that are only divisible by themselves and 1. You know, things like 2, 5, and $2^{77,232,917} - 1$.

Primes are the coolest because they've been super useful in modern encryption technologies. It's pretty easy to choose two prime numbers and multiply them together to get a result, right? But given only the resulting number, it's much harder to figure out which primes were multiplied together to get it. So the "prime factors" of very large numbers are perfect for use as ultra-secure decryption keys. It took three MIT scientists and a whole lot of Manischewitz at a Passover Seder one year to figure this out, but their famous RSA cryptosystem is now used all over the internet.

That's something I wish more people understood about math. It's not just dry numbers on paper. It's teamwork! It's passion! It's puzzle-solving! It's too much terrible sweet wine (not recommended for mathematicians under 21-years of age)!

To that end, The Master Theorem Games (TMT's board gaming wing) recently released a family-friendly math game called Proof!™ to show people that math can and should be a group bonding endeavor. It's pretty simple; from a layout of nine number cards, players race to create equations using as many +, -, x, ÷, and √ symbols as they need. For example: If you had the cards 3, 10 and 13, you could create the equation 3 + 10 = 13, or the cards 2, 4, 7, and 1 could become 2 + 4 = 7 - 1.

There's also a trickier online version of the game that I update with weekly challenges for people just like you. Challenge #34 is my all-time favorite. Solve it here or online, but the answer this time will simply be an equation rather than a word or phrase. Sometimes, math speaks for itself.

This is today,

M

Hints: 115 • **Solution:** 192

Make an equation resulting in $\frac{667}{1271}$

29

69

99

58

82

62

46

41

93

$+$ $-$ $\times$ $\div$ $\sqrt{}$

The Building Blocks of Life

August 4

Whenever I'm hanging in my decked-out nerd cave of a basement, I'm usually doing one of a few things: a) writing puzzles, b) listening to music, or c) playing with Legos.

Some people might not get why a grown person would be so into Legos. What they don't understand is that these little pieces can be so much more than mere toys. They can be towers. They can be castles. They can be Death Stars! They contain all you need to build almost anything from the ground up.

I got into Legos when I was a kid, but even now I sometimes use them to model out future puzzles, philosophical ideas, even real-life construction plans.

You know what I mean?

This is today,
M

Hints: 115 • **Solution:** 194

L1

L2

L3

L4

L5

L6

Nothing to See Here

January 31

In my ample free time, I like to dabble in photography (in addition to hanging out in my garden, writing mystery novels, documenting the inner workings of my mind, and playing video games, of course).

I've cultivated some pretty sweet photography skills over my years of touring the world. (I always manage to squeeze in some sightseeing between infiltrating the mob and brokering peace between rogue nations.) The thing I'm most proud of is the way I've learned to frame objects in beautiful, unusual ways. You have to try to find the right light, the right coloring, the right ambient effects.

In other words, I think Photoshop and auto-filter apps like Instagram are copouts. Photoshop has a time and a place—like when you're trying to create something that looks fantastical on purpose—but there's nothing to see in photos that use silly filters to give drama and depth to otherwise bland images. Other than examining the clever algorithms behind those filters, of course, there's no real substance there worth seeing.

Sadly, there are countless photos out there full of saccharine false nostalgia. They may seem full of emotion, but when I look at them, I don't see much of anything at all.

This is today,
M

Hints: 115 • **Solution:** 196

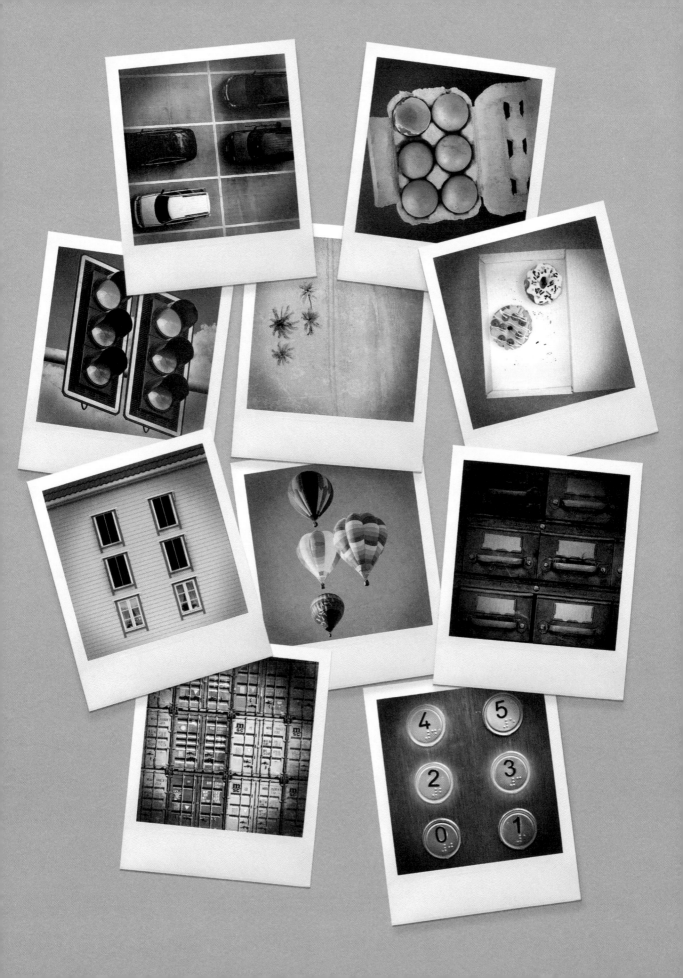

In Memoriam

Memories make us who we are. Everything I learned as an undergrad studying astrophysics. Everywhere I went while on missions for an agency that will remain unnamed. And everyone I've met along the way. I remember them all, more or less, and each of those memories mean the world to me, and have formed me into the dazzling creature you have come to know and love.

But sometimes something happens that you want to forget. Sometimes you make a mistake. Sometimes, in the business that I'm in, you miss a piece of intelligence and something terrible happens. And even though you should always remember everything leading up to that mistake to keep it from happening again—sometimes your brain just wants to erase that entire memory's existence.

I don't make many mistakes. But the ones I have made are like ghosts in the periphery of my brain. It's hard to explain the weird ways my mind indexes into those memories. The places I've been, things I've seen, and people I've met and let down zip around the neurons in my head as a vague hodgepodge of disorderly memories. To cope, when I recall snippets of those things, I write them down in my journal so I can eventually disentangle them and get at the actual person, place, or thing.

To paraphrase a famous quote, only by remembering the past can we keep it from repeating itself.

This is today,

M

I remember taking a van to go see a swirly black and blue painting.

_ _ _ _

I remember a tennis player from another planet.

_ _ _

I remember a man who was over the moon for his big biceps.

_ _ _

I remember a triumphant structure near the champs.

_ _ _ _

I remember a tall, liberating woman who always reached for the sky.

_ _ _ _

I remember identical brothers in a city of insomniacs.

_ _ _

I remember a civil man of royal character.

_ _ _ _

I remember a civil woman in a field of red flowers.

_ _

I remember a tropical paradise with eggs hidden behind mysterious statues.

_ _ _

_ _ _ _ _ _

Is Anyone Out There?

November 16

Back in my NASA days I worked on a little project called the Arecibo message with my colleagues Frank Drake and Carl Sagan. A humble transmission less than three minutes long, it was one of humanity's first attempts at sending a message to alien civilizations.

But we obviously couldn't send a message to our galactic brethren in any earthly language. As cool as spoken words can be, they're nothing more than made up grunts that only have meaning to those who already know what they symbolize. In other words: I'd bet you my screen-ready Chewbacca costume from the original Star Wars trilogy that aliens don't speak English.

No, we realized that to really make a connection, we'd need to include depictions of universal truths such as atoms, molecules, and planets—things all intelligent inhabitants of the universe would be familiar with—and then gradually build up a message from that foundation.

But here's the rub: we haven't heard anything back yet. Some scientists are starting to think it's possible there may not be anyone out there at all. But I prefer to believe we were just noobs at making a message that aliens could easily understand and it simply went right over their heads (or thoraxes or antennae or whatever).

So, I've been sharpening my universal message making skills since then. In preparation for sending another big ol' Hello to the stars, I made a test message that should at least be easy for TMT members and their ilk to understand.

Look, you were the closest thing to an alien that I could find.

This is today,
M

Hints: 116 • **Solution:** 200

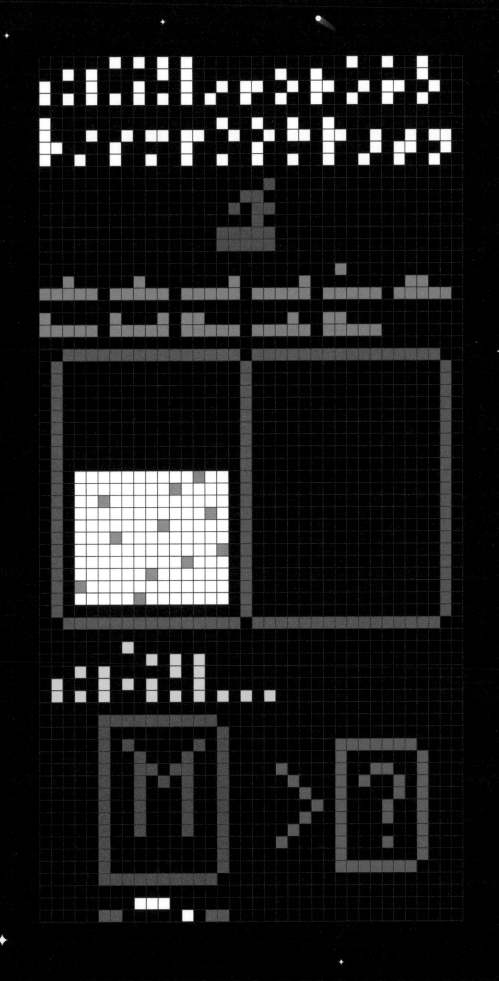

Telescope Telemarketers

Ever since I bought my tremendous new telescope to help me search for exoplanets, I've encountered an entirely unexpected problem: Did you know that telescope companies employ telemarketers?

I asked these telemarketers to stop calling me, but they won't leave me alone. They're always trying to sell me a bigger mirror or better spectrometer. So, I decided to take matters into my own hands. I hacked into their computer system in order to find their CEO's phone number so that I could keep calling and harassing *him* at dinner time.

When I got in, all I could find were some random employees' phone numbers, and the data looked corrupted anyway. I was close to giving up when I noticed that the CEO's number was actually cleverly concealed within those corrupted digits. Those telemarketers might be annoying, but you've gotta give 'em some credit.

This is today,

M

Hints: 117 • **Solution:** 202

```
m@themastermachine:~$ ssh-add ~/.ssh/stolen_ttm_key
Identity added: /Users/m/.ssh/stolen_ttm_key (m/.ssh/stolen_tt-
m_key)
m@themastermachine:~$ ssh root@telescope-telemarketing.com
The authenticity of host 'telescope-telemarketing.com'
(87.54.1.9) can't be established.
RSA key fingerprint is
a5:67:9f:3e:e1:18:77:3b:ba:81:b9:31:a8:a2:e2:22.
Are you sure you want to continue connecting (yes/no)? yes
Warning: Permanently added 'telescope-telemarket-
ing.com,87.54.1.9' (RSA) to the list of known hosts.
root@telescope-telemarketing.com:~# history | grep psql
  129 psql -d ttm_db -U admin --command 'select * from customers'
  149 psql -d ttm_db -U admin --command 'select phone_numbers
from employees'
  170 history | grep psql
root@telescope-telemarketing.com:~# !149
   phone_number
```

786-*23-6837
33*-765-474*
278-766-6637

```
root@telescope-telemarketing.com:~#
```

Get Your Kicks

July 4

Over the July Fourth holiday, I drove along Route 66 en route to a meeting with colleagues to discuss some nearby UFO sightings.

This storied route may have been a bit out of my way, but I had a hankering to delve into the history surrounding one of the most famous roads in the United States. As you may have heard, "it winds from Chicago to L.A., more than 2,000 miles all the way." What better time to explore some Americana than on America's birthday?

Of course, everything looks very different now than in the route's heyday, but—if you'll allow me a touch of poetic license—I caught a whiff of the past in the dust, could almost make out the shape of the people, businesses, and culture that used to consider this thoroughfare its lifeline. Smells of sweet apple pie wafting from mom and pop diners. Snippets of pleasantries exchanged at filling stations.

When I finally finished my drive down Route 66 and started my journey towards the nearby interstate, I looked up to find a road sign that perfectly encapsulated the nostalgia surrounding this legendary route.

This is today,

M

Hints: 117 • **Solution:** 204

ROUTE 66

ROADSIDE ATTRACTION!

O L K T H E L R
T F E I O E O H
E M H R D A R T

Words Words Words

When I was brushing up on my Japanese a few years ago to help decrypt encoded transmissions between Japan and North Korea, I was continually struck by one glorious fact: aside from a handful of irregular verbs, Japanese grammar is mostly consistent, and all of the phonetic letters actually sound like they're supposed to.

It's not like French or even English, where there are lots of annoying exceptions to every rule. Not to badmouth any language out there; I love language—the human ability to communicate complex concepts through a series of sounds—and I love playing with the subtle relationships between words and meanings.

I just feel bad for non-native English speakers who get caught in the labyrinth of pronunciation and grammar rules that aren't even internally consistent. You can't blame them for wanting to call the whole thing off and sticking with their original languages. Maybe we should all switch to Japanese?

This is today,
M

Hints: 118 • **Solution:** 206

1. Bob didn't realize the shoes he bought were so expensive. "Ght," he moaned as he looked at his credit card bill.

2. Sally climbed all the way to the top of the plateau, only to find it was crawling with bugs. "Eau!" she screamed. "It's gross up here!"

3. John joined in singing a hymn with his congregation. "Mn..." he hummed in perfect unison with the group.

4. Michelle discovered that her neighbor had stolen her power drill from her garage. "Eigh!" she yelled. "Give it back!"

5. General George scoffed upon receipt of the enemy's surrender message. "Pt!" George spit on the ground in disgust. "We refuse to acknowledge your surrender!"

6. Chris went to get out some dough to make pizza for dinner. "Ough," he said disappointedly. "It's gone bad already!"

King of the Court

August 31

You've heard of Ultimate Frisbee, right? Well, my favorite form of exercise is something even cooler: Ultimate Four Square—you know, that game from your grade school playground that involved bouncing a ball between (you guessed it) four squares?

Here's a refresher. The King in square 1 gets the game started by bouncing the ball to another square. The player in that square needs to then use only his or her hands to smack the ball towards someone else. Miss, or bounce the ball out of the four suare court, and you're out.

When I was King, I'd like to get a little crazy and dip into the alternate rulebook. No matter what variation we'd play, though, the keys to the game were always speed and accuracy. If I kept those in mind, I was golden.

Naturally, I was stoked to be a special guest commentator at last year's Four Square World Championships. The final match started typically enough with players P1, P2, P3, and P4 standing ready in squares 1 - 4 respectively. P1 served the ball as usual, but what happened next between P2 and P3 felt like it belonged at Wimbledon.

After that epic showdown, P1 and P4 had a similar back-and-forth before P1 fell to a cherry bomb, was dethroned, and a new King was crowned.

Move over Williams sisters.

This is today,
M

...and the game is officially underway! The ball first lands all the way at the top of P2's square just to the left of center. P2 bounces the ball to P3 just a little below dead center of her square. P3 masterfully smacks it back to the very-hard-to-reach bottom left corner. But P2 dives just in time to hit it back to P3 yet again, just to the right of where it had landed before. P3 hits it right back to P2, just above where it landed before. P2 now lobs it back into the very top of P3's square, just to the right of center. P3 returns it just below dead center, and P2 slaps it just slightly above the very bottom left corner of P3's square... wow, what a game so far, folks!

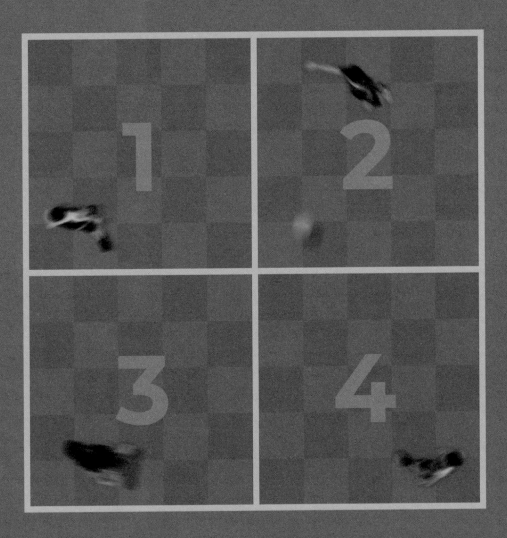

The Art of the Written Word

Books are the keys to all knowledge. They help you learn about the world, and they can even help you learn about yourself. That's sort of the point of fiction, I think. To impart hidden wisdoms when you think you're just whiling away an hour or two.

That's why I just had to write a few myself. I've learned a lot through my long and storied life, and I wanted share some of those lessons with you. My preferred storytelling vehicle is the murder mystery, as you've seen in these pages, because—well, they're sort of the ultimate puzzle!

The best books (and I'd like to think the things I write fall into that category) are a source of knowledge and entertainment, but also intrigue and subtle subtext. If you pay close enough attention to the pages flipping by, you may guess at the ending, but hopefully the journey will still thrill you.

Take a look, it's in a book, as they say.

This is today,
M

The Master Institute of Technology

Here we are, dear puzzlers. At the end. It's been a wild ride, full of murder mysteries and music and animals and Legos and stars and the universe. Pretty epic. I must say I'm proud of you for making it this far, but reaching our last Theorem has made me feel nostalgic. So I'd like to share one more tidbit of my past with you.

Some of the most rewarding years of my life (not including the time we've spent together, of course) was when I was a student at MIT. I studied in a little-known research lab that sought to create pie-in-the-sky technologies, the likes of which would have made Ben Franklin and Thomas Edison giddy.

It was an amazing time of exploration and learning. During my tenure there, I had access to mouth-watering technologies like 3D printers, laser cutters, milling machines—a veritable Wonka-like wonderland of tech and imagination. It really made me appreciate how we got here as a society, how much hard work went into all the old-school, but world-changing technologies that came before.

Perhaps the best thing about MIT, though, was the people. It was incredible being part of an entire community of brilliant people who valued making things, who loved puzzles (want to join my team for next year's Mystery Hunt, anyone?), who thought deeply about the future, and who sincerely enjoyed all sorts of unique, nerdy pursuits.

Sound familiar? In many ways, I've modeled TMT after MIT—both a global network of smart people with incredible skills, looking to change the world. And after you solve this final Theorem, I think we can officially say you've earned your degree.

I can already imagine the cheesy ads plastered all over the subway...

This is today, tomorrow, and always,
M

Hints: 119 • **Solution:** 212

17 REASONS

WHY YOU SHOULD EARN YOUR DEGREE AT THE
THE MASTER INSTITUTE OF TECHNOLOGY

1 We've got the world's only robotic professor that runs on auto and teaches everything from Big O notation to how to extract bile from lab rats!

2 You can take any of our 812 eco-conscious courses, including one that famously explains how a single flower stem can power an engine for over 150 miles!

3 Our faculty includes dozens of amazing celebrities, such as Patrick Ewing, who runs our state-of-the-art machine shop!

4 Sick of math? Simply get any intern from our student center to help calculate the value of e for you!

5 Our world-class botanists will take you on frequent field trips to the nearby forest where you'll learn about every type of fir out there!

6 All our interns come with 10 fingers so you'll never have to compute anything on yours again!

7 We've got as great a financial aid package to comp your studies as you could possibly hope for!

8 We've also got totally rad on-campus music groups. O, and free music lessons, too!

9 There's a luxury cot in every room with a convenient pouch to hold your gin and tonic!

10 We offer classes on tele-marketing that teach you to hone your salesmanship skills!

11 Loved learning about all those firs? Our wonderful botanists will also give you lots of light but amazing reading material on Bacterial Leaf Blight (BLB)

12 Your tuition includes free trips to the ER just in case you blow something up in the lab!

13 Running a lot of servers? We give out 10 IP addresses per student!

14 A huge perk of living on campus is our fun slides between every floor that'll make you yell, "Whee!"

15 You'll find a pen in every desk and a window cill situated in every dorm room!

16 Don't want to get out of bed? Take one of our many tele-presence classes remotely, such as our one on Microsoft Visio!

17 Your tuition also includes the ability to print out up to 1000 pages per day in our lab with the simple press of a button!

YOU WON'T KNOW WHAT YOU'RE MISSING OUT ON UNTIL YOU'RE HERE. ENROLL TODAY AND EARN OUR MOST COVETED DEGREE!

Hints

"People who think they know
everything are a great annoyance
to those of us who do."

Isaac Asimov

TRAINING THEOREM: PRACTICE MAKES PERFECT

HINT 1: Qdldladq, H khjd trhmf qdc sn ldzm, "Gdx, knnj gdqd enq sgd ehmzk zmrvdq."

HINT 2: Sgd szkj zants mtladqr zmc sgd zkogzads hr z bktd sgzs xnt rgntkc ad bnmudqshmf adsvddm mtladqr zmc kdssdqr.

HINT 3: Cn sgzs. Bnmudqs dzbg ne sgd qdc mtladqr sn kdssdqr, vgdqd Z hr 1, A hr 2, zmc rn nm.

TRAINING THEOREM: ELOQUENT ARTICULATION

HINT 1: Sgdrd HMCDW bzqcr dzbg gzud z vnqc zmc z mtladq nm sgdl.

HINT 2: Sgdqd zqd 5 vnqcr zmc 5 qdc akzmjr zs anssnl, rn sqx dwsqzbshmf nmd kdssdq odq vnqc sn ots hm dzbg ne sgd akzmjr.

HINT 3: Trd sgd mtladq nm dzbg hmcdw bzqc sn "hmcdw" hmsn sgd vnqc nm sgzs bzqc. Enq dwzlokd, sgd 9sg kdssdq ne BNMSDLOKZSD hr zm Z. Jddo fnhmf. Vgzs cndr sgzs rodkk?

TRAINING THEOREM: STRAIGHT TO THE TOP

HINT 1: Gnv bntkc xnt zqqzmfd sgd kdssdqr nm sgdrd okzxhmf bzqcr sn rodkk sgd rnktshnm?

HINT 2: Nqcdq sgd bzqcr ax sgd mtladq ne rxlankr nm sgdl, vgdqd Z, vhsg nmd chzlnmc, hr ehqrs zmc M, vhsg ehud gdzqsr, hr kzrs.

HINT 3: Fqnto sgd bzqcr ax rths rn sgzs chzlnmcr lzjd to sgd ehqrs vnqc zmc gdzqsr sgd rdbnmc.

TRAINING THEOREM: WHAT'S YOUR SIGN?

HINT 1: Vgzs jhmc ne "rhfmr" bntkc sgdrd ad?

HINT 2: Sgdrd zqd ynchzb rhfmr. Mns rtqd vghbg hr vghbg? Eddk eqdd sn knnj hs to.

HINT 3: Vqhsd sgd mzld ne dzbg ynchzb rhfm hm sgd rozbdr mdws sn hsr rxlank zmc otkk nts sgd qdc kdssdqr. Vgzs cndr sgzs rodkk?

TRAINING THEOREM: BEWARE THE IDES OF MARCH

HINT 1: Sgdqd zqd z vgnkd atmbg ne bnllnm bhogdqr nts sgdqd, khjd rtarshstshnm bhogdqr, Lnqrd bncd, rdlzognqdr, entq-rptzqd, Okzxezhq, ohfodm, qntsd, zmc dudm Bzdrzq bhogdqr.

HINT 2: H szkj zants sghr ftx Bzdrzq z kns, rn xnt'c ad vhrd sn ftdrr sghr hr z Bzdrzq rghes bhogdq. Ats ax gnv ltbg rgntkc xnt rghes sgd kdssdqr hm sgd hlzfd?

HINT 3: Rghes sgd kdssdqr hm sgd hlzfd cnvm ax 4, ldzmhmf Y adbnldr U, H adbnldr D, zmc rn nm. Vgzs cn xnt fds?

1. THE MASTER THEOREM

HINT 1: Dzbg ptnszshnm qdedqr sn sgd ehqrs khmd ne z fqdzs vnqj, ad hs z mnudk, ondl nq okzx.

HINT 2: Nmbd xnt'ud trdc sgd ehqrs, nq "nodmhmf," kdssdqr ne dzbg vnqj sn rodkk nts z ehmzk ptnszshnm, sghmj zants sgzs nodmhmf khmd zmc sgd dmcdzunq hs adfhmr.

HINT 3: "H zl gdqd." Vgdqd gzud H rddm sgzs adenqd? Snczx? Hm sghr annj odqgzor?

2. MASTERS OF MANY THEOREMS

HINT 1: Sghr hr z oqdssx rszmczqc fdnldsqx oqnakdl, vhsg z Lzrsdq Sgdnqdl svhrs. Zmc xnt'kk gzud sn lzrsdq z ozqshbtkzq sgdnqdl sn rnkud hs.

HINT 2: Bnmudqs dzbg mnm-qdc kdssdq hmsn hsr zkogzmtldqhb uzktd zmc trd sgd Oxsgzfnqdzm sgdnqdl (z² + a² = b²) sn rnkud enq sgd qdc Wr. Mnsd sgzs lzsbghmf shbj lzqjr ldzmr sgnrd khmdr zqd sgd rzld kdmfsg.

HINT 3: Mnv tmcn vgzs xnt chc adenqd—stqm sgd uzktdr ne sgd qdc Wr azbj hmsn kdssdqr.

3. EMINENT MS

HINT 1: Ehmc sgd 11 "hlonrsnqr" nm sghr khrs sgzs zqd rodkkdc vhsg z ehqrs kdssdq ne L, ats rntkcm's ad. H'c enqfhud xnt enq Fnnfkhmf he mddcdc.

HINT 2: Ehftqd nts sgd kdssdqr sgzs sgnrd mzldr rgntkc rszqs vhsg. Chc xnt vhmc to vhsg fhaadqhrg? Sgnrd hlonrsnqr bdqszhmkx zqd rghesx.

HINT 3: Rn xnt'ud fns UYYADFMXUFK, zmc xnt jmnv xnt mddc sn rghes sgnrd kdssdqr. Ats ax vgzs zlntms, xnt zrj? Vdkk, rnldshldr H bzm ad z ahs uzhm, rn sqx rgheshmf ax L, nq 13.

4. DIFFERENT

HINT 1: Nmd ne sgdrd sghmfr hr mns khjd sgd nsgdqr... Vghbg hlzfd hm dzbg fqnto hr cheedqdms eqnl sgd nsgdq sgqdd?

HINT 2: Fqnto 1 sno qhfgs: Knrs vdhfgs. Fqnto 2 knvdq kdes: Rsqhjd nts. Fqnto 3 sno kdes: Z-rgzqo. Fqnto 4 knvdq kdes: Lhkk. Fqnto 5 sno kdes: Sgqdd ohdbd rths. Fqnto 6 knvdq kdes: Szjd nee.

HINT 3: Fqnto 1: knrs ur. vnm. Fqnto 2: nts ur. hm. Fqnto 3: bnmrnmzmsr ur.

unvdk. Fqnto 4: qgxlhmf vnqcr ur. mnm-qgxlhmf vnqc. Fqnto 5: mtladqr ur. kdssdq. Fqnto 6: nee ur. nm.

5. WHAT HATH GOD WROUGHT?

HINT 1: Sgd ogqzrd hm sgd otyykd hr z ptnsd. Vgn rzhc hs? Vgzs chc sgzs odqrnm bqdzsd?

HINT 2: Sgnrd vdqd Rzltdk Lnqrd'r ehqrs vnqcr nm sgd sdkdfqzog. Lnqrd bncd hmunkudr z rdqhdr ne cnsr zmc czrgdr, vghbg zqd rgnqs zmc knmf rdfldmsr. Qdlhmc xnt ne zmxsghmf?

HINT 3: Sgd rgnqs zmc knmf cqhor qdoqdrdms cnsr zmc czrgdr hm Lnqrd bncd. Trd dzbg kdssdq hm "vqntfgs" sn rdozqzsd kdssdqr hm sgd ehmzk zmrvdq. Enq dwzlokd, sgd svn czrgdr tmcdq sgd V sqzmrkzsd sn zm L.

6. L.M. ENTARRIE

HINT 1: Vgn rzhc sgzs ptnsd zants z "qdhfm ne nqcdq"?

HINT 2: Qdzc sghr rsnqx zr zm zkkdfnqx enq sgd Odqhnchb Szakd. Otkk to z bgzqs zmc knnj enq z fqnto ne "gnnkhfzmr" sgzs khudr mdzq z ezlhkx ne "mnakd" dkdldmsr.

HINT 3: Vghbg dkdldmsr khud nm Qntsd (Fqnto) 17 adsvddm dwhsr (zsnlhb mtladqr) 9 sgqntfg 85?

7. EFFIN' WEB SERVICES

HINT 1: O hr ntq qdrhcdms chqsx-lntsg. Cn xnt rdd gnv zmfqx gd fns?

HINT 2: O rodmcr z kns ne shld zs ghr jdxanzqc.

HINT 3: Sgd rxlankr hm O'r oqnezmhsx bzm ad entmc nm sgd rzld jdxanzqc jdxr zr 0 - 9 (sqdzs sgd rkzrg zr z rozbd). Bnmudqs sgd rxlankr sn sgdhq

bnqqdronmchmf mtladqr, sgdm bnmudqs sgnrd sn kdssdqr.

8. WRITTEN IN THE STARCH

HINT 1: Enq fdmdqzshnmr, gtlzmr gzud knnjdc enq ozssdqmr hm sgd bnrlnr.

HINT 2: Knnj enq ozssdqmr adsvddm sgd edzstqdr ne dzbg rszq zmc sgd

bncd mzldr H bgnrd enq sgdl. Mnsd sgzs sgdqd zqd ehud edzstqdr enq

dzbg rszq zmc ehud kdssdqr hm dzbg bncd mzld.

HINT 3: Sgd ehqrs kdssdq ne sgd rszq bnknq hr sgd ehqrs kdssdq ne sgd

bncd mzld. Sgd chrszmbd hm 10^{10} khfgs xdzqr hr sgd kzrs kdssdq ne sgd

bncd mzld. Jddo fnhmf. Vgzs rgntkc sgd bncd mzld ne sgd ehmzk rszq ad?

9. OLD MCDONALD

HINT 1: Sgd chqdbshnmr MV, MD, RV, zmc RD qdedq sn sgd onrhshnmr ne

dzbg ohf odm nm sgd aktdoqhmsr.

HINT 2: Trd sgd bzqchmzk chqdbshnmr mnqsg (M), rntsg (R), dzrs (D), zmc

vdrs (V) sn bnknq hm sgd ohf odm vzkkr. B ldzmr bdmsdq. Bntkc sgzs ad z

bncd?

HINT 3: Nmd ldsgnc ne dmbnchmf sghmfr hr sgd ohfodm bhogdq. Eddk

eqdd sn knnj hs to.

10. MOVE TO THE BEAT

HINT 1: He xnt cnm's jmnv gnv sn qdzc ltrhb, ehmc z aqhde oqhldq

nmkhmd. Enbtr nm tmcdqrszmchmf vghbg khmdr bnqqdronmc vhsg vghbg

mnsdr zmc gnv lzmx adzsr dzbg sxod ne mnsd fdsr.

HINT 2: Sghmj ne dzbg mnsd'r kdssdq zr hsr zkogzmtldqhb uzktd. Enq dwzlokd, zm Z mnsd vntkc ad 1. Vgdm xnt rdd z bgnqc, zcc sgd uzktdr ne sgd hmchuhctzk mnsd snfdsgdq.

HINT 3: Ltkshokx sgd zkogzmtldqhb uzktd ne dzbg mnsd (nq bgnqc) ax sgd mtladq ne adzsr hs fdsr, zrrtlhmf z vgnkd mnsd fdsr entq.

11. WHAT SOME PEOPLE CALL FATE

HINT 1: "Vgzs zqd sgd nccr" sgzs H'c otkk z lzqakd ne sghr bnknq eqnl z azf ne sgdrd bnknqdc lzqakdr?

HINT 2: Sgd oqnazahkhsx ne otkkhmf z rhmfkd akzbj lzqakd nts ne z azf vhsg 3 aktd, 4 qdc, 1 akzbj, zmc 5 nqzmfd lzqakdr hr 1 nts ne (3 + 4 + 1 + 5), nq 1 / 13. Mnv szjd z rsza zs sgd qdrs.

HINT 3: Lx ozqzkkdk qdzkhshdr gzud z kns "hm bnllnm", rn sqx fhuhmf zkk sgd eqzbshnmr xnt bnld to vhsg z bnllnm cdmnlhmzsnq. Lzxad...26?

12. TURING TEST

HINT 1: Sghr hr z sxohbzk knfhb otyykd. Rszqs vhsg Lzwhlhkhzm zmc zrrtld gd'r z gtlzm. Bnmshmtd vnqjhmf eqnl sgzs zrrtloshnm zmc rdd vgdqd hs fdsr xnt.

HINT 2: Enkknv sgd sqzhk zmc jddo lzjhmf zrrtloshnmr tmshk xnt ghs z knfhbzk bnmsqzchbshnm. Azbjsqzbj vgdm xnt mddc sn zmc qduhrd xntq zrrtloshnmr tmshk dudqxsghmf dudqxnmd rzxr hr bnmrhrsdms.

HINT 3: Mnsd sgzs dzbg mzld hr dwzbskx sdm kdssdqr knmf zmc sgdqd zqd dwzbskx sdm rtaidbsr. Mnv "hmsdqqnfzsd sgd gtlzmr" ax hmcdwhmf hmsn sgdhq mzldr sn fds sgd ehmzk zmrvdq.

13. QUANTUM DUPLICITY

HINT 1: Sghmj ne sgd vnqcr hm sgd hlzfd zr zsnlr, zmc sgdhq kdssdqr zr rtazsnlhb ozqshbkdr.

HINT 2: Qdldladq: H sghmj sgzs sgd lnrs hmsdqdrshmf zrodbs ne ptzmstl ldbgzmhbr hr gnv sgd rzld rtazsnlhb ozqshbkd bzm ad hm svn okzbdr zs nmbd.

HINT 3: Mnshbd sgzs dzbg vnqc hm sgd hlzfd gzr dwzbskx nmd kdssdq, nq rtazsnlhb ozqshbkd, sgzs zoodzqr svhbd. Zmc sgzs sgd mtladq ne "dkdbsqnmr" zqntmc dzbg vnqc qzmfdr eqnl 1 sn 10.

14. 8-BIT CLASSICS

HINT 1: Xnt cnm's mddc sn hcdmshex dzbg ne sgd fzldr hm sgdrd hlzfdr. Hmrsdzc, ozx zssdmshnm sn lx szkj zants sgd ahmzqx chrshmbshnmr adsvddm to/cnvm zmc nm/nee.

HINT 2: Gnv vntkc rnldnmd bnmudqs 8-ahs ahmzqx bncd sn kdssdqr? Vgx cnm's xnt zrj Fnnfkd?

HINT 3: Dzbg uhcdn fzld hlzfd bnmbdzkr z rdqhdr ne dhfgs 0'r zmc 1'r. Sghmj ne "nm" nq "to" zr 1, zmc "nee" nq "cnvm" zr 0. Sgdm bnmudqs dzbg 8-ahs bncd sn z kdssdq trhmf zm "ZRBHH" szakd.

15. THE FINAL REVELATION

HINT 1: Shld sn bdmsqzkhyd xntq sghmjhmf.

HINT 2: Rdd gnv sgnrd okzbd mzldr qzchzsd nts eqnl sgd bdmsdq ne sgd lzo?

HINT 3: Ehmc sgd bdmsdq kdssdq hm dzbg vnqc. Ots sgdl hm nqcdq rszqshmf zs sgd bdmsdq ne sgd lzo zmc fnhmf ntsvzqc, zmc xnt'kk fds xntq nvm odqrnmzk ehmzk qdudkzshnm.

16. SLEEP IS THE STATION GRAND

HINT 1: Sghmj ne lx cnnckd zr z "lzyd" ne mdtqnmr.

HINT 2: Mzuhfzsd eqnl sno kdes sn anssnl qhfgs vhsgnts ghsshmf zmx cdzc dmcr. Xnt bzmmns qtm bnmshmtntrkx sgqntfg knmf ogqzrdr—itrs bnmmdbs ghfgkhfgsdc vnqcr sn dzbg nsgdq uhz khmdr.

HINT 3: Rsqhmf snfdsgdq zkk sgd vnqcr xnt ohbj to zknmf sgd vzx. Rntmcr jhmcz ondshb, cndrm's hs? Vgdqd'r hs eqnl?

17. WHO IN THE WHERE WITH THE WHAT

HINT 1: Sgd uhbshl'r mzld hr Lq. Anccx. Vgn hr sgzs?

HINT 2: Sgd rsnqx hr zm zkktrhnm sn sgd bkzrrhb lxsdqx anzqc fzld Bktd. He xnt cnm's jmnv gnv sn okzx, fn sdzbg xntqrdke. Enbtr nm sgd nqhfhmzk anzqc fzld, mns sgnrd mdvdq nmdr.

HINT 3: Knnj enq qdedqdmbdr sn dzbg ne sgd rtrodbsr, vdzonmr, zmc qnnlr eqnl sgd nqhfhmzk anzqc fzld. Sgd fzld hr z oqnbdrr ne dkhlhmzshnm, rn vgzs lhfgs xnt ad knnjhmf enq gdqd?

18. GEOCACHING

HINT 1: Trd Fnnfkd Dzqsg nq "rzsdkkhsd" uhdv nm Fnnfkd Lzor sn dwoknqd sgd okzbdr zs sgdrd bnnqchmzsdr. Mn mddc sn sxod sgd ° nq ' nq " rxlankr, rhmbd hs'kk jmnv vgzs xnt ldzm vhsgnts sgnrd. Enq dwzlokd, 37 58 17.35M, 23 43 35.90D vntkc vnqj itrs ehmd.

HINT 2: Dzbg FOR bnnqchmzsd ohmonhmsr z ezlntr kzmclzqj. Ehmc sgd hmenqlzshnm qdptdrsdc zants dzbg kzmclzqj zmc rdd vgzs xnt bzm cn vhsg hs.

HINT 3: He xnt'qd mns trhmf Fnnfkd Dzqsg nq Lzor, xnt lhfgs mddc sn cn z khsskd nmkhmd chffhmf sn ehmc sgd hmen qdptdrsd. Oktf sgd zmrvdqr sn dzbg qhcckd hmsn sgd ehmzk dptzshnm. Vgdqd cndr sgzs szjd xnt?

19. SHIFTY FINANCIAL BUSINESS

HINT 1: Sgdrd shbjdq rxlankr zqd to nq cnvm bdqszhm zlntmsr eqnl vgzs sgdx vdqd adenqd.

HINT 2: Gnv ltbg sgdrd "rghesx" rsnbjr vdqd to nq cnvm zmc vgdm ozhmsr zm hmsdqdrshmf rsnqx ne vgzs'r addm fnhmf nm nudq shld.

HINT 3: Aqhmf sgd rsnbjr azbj sn sgdhq nqhfhmzk uzktdr ax rgheshmf sgd kdssdqr hm dzbg shbjdq rxlank ax sgd noonrhsd zlntms hs gzc bgzmfdc. Sgdm zqqzmfd sgdl ax czsd.

20. OF SIBERIA, WORD PARTS, AND YOU

HINT 1: Ehmc sgd nmd, bnllnm vnqc hm dmfkhrg sgzs bnmszhmr dzbg kdssdq rdptdmbd zr z vgnkd, vhsgnts zmx nsgdq kdssdqr adsvddm sgdl. Enq dwzlokd, KOE bzm ad entmc hm GDKOETK, khjd sghr ghms.

HINT 2: COD - z ozqshbtkzqkx mnhrx ahqc. OVQ - sgd Ktrhszmhz nq Shszmhb, enq dwzlokd.

Cipher Text:	A	B	C	D	E	F	G	H	I	J	K	L	M	N	O	P	Q	R	S	T	U	V	W	X	Y	Z
Plain Text:	B	C	D	E	F	G	H	I	J	K	L	M	N	O	P	Q	R	S	T	U	V	W	X	Y	Z	A

HINT 3: NXQ - vgzs xnt lhfgs cn vhsg z rsnkdm bnmudqshakd. HSO - sn onhms nts lhmnq ekzvr. EVZ - bnloqnlhrd ax lddshmf gdqd.

21. ANCIENT CROSSWORDS

HINT 1: Trd sgd nqhfhmzk Rzsnq Rptzqd zr z aktdoqhms sn tmrbqzlakd lx udqrhnm.

HINT 2: Szjd sgd kdssdqr hm lx rptzqd eqnl sgd rzld onrhshnmr zr sgnrd hm sgd nqhfhmzk rptzqd trdc sn rodkk "Ozsdq Mnrsdq" (nm z ehqrs bnld ehqrs rdqud azrhr). Enq dwzlokd, sgd L hm lx rptzqd hr vgdqd sgd O vzr hm sgd nqhfhmzk.

HINT 3: Mn, "lzcd fnckhjd" hr mns sgd ehmzk zmrvdq. Sqdzs sghr khjd z bqnrrvnqc bktd enq sgd ehmzk zmrvdq. Zmc jddo sgd sgdld ne ozkhmcqnldr hm lhmc.

22. RECURSIVE: ADJ. SEE RECURSIVE

HINT 1: Sghmj ne sghr fqhc ne kdssdqr khjd z fqzog, zmc trd ozhqr ne kdssdqr zr WX bnnqchmzsdr. Mnv vghbg kdssdqr lhfgs xnt trd?

HINT 2: Sgd Sgdnqdl shskd hr hm z udqx bnlotsdqx enms, hrm's hs? Sqx trhmf sgnrd kdssdqr zr xntq hmhshzk hmotsr. Z sho sn fds xnt rszqsdc: (Q,D) hr sgd ehqrs WX bnnqchmzsd, vghbg kzmcr nm zm H hm sgd fqhc.

HINT 3: Sghr hr z qdbtqrhud otyykd, rn HMEHMHSD KNNO hrm's sgd ehmzk zmrvdq. Jddo fnhmf... Vgzs xnt fds rddlr sn ad zrjhmf: Vgx cndrm's qdbtqrhnm knno enqdudq? Cnm's jmnv? Zrj Vhjhodchz.

23. BIRDS, BEES, AND STRANGE AMALGAMS

HINT 1: Hcdmshex sgd svn zmhlzkr hm dzbg fqnto ne hlzfdr. Rzx sgdhq mzldr nts kntc, nmd zmc sgdm sgd nsgdq. Mnshbd zmxsghmf hmsdqdrshmf?

HINT 2: He xnt bnlahmd sgd "bnllnm," nq bnkknpthzk, mzld ne sgd zmhlzkr hm dzbg fqnto, xnt fds sgd bnllnm mzld ne xds zmnsgdq zmhlzk. Mnv, ots sgdl hm "nqcdq."

HINT 3: Ehmc sgd rbhdmshehb bkzrrhehbzshnm enq sgd nqcdq ne dzbg zlzkfzl. (Enq dwzlokd, sgd rohcdq lnmjdx hr ne sgd nqcdq "Oqhlzsdr.")

24. PRECISION PAINTBALL

HINT 1: H ldmshnm sgzs lx bqxosnfqzogdq eqhdmcr cnm's sghmj H okzx ezhq. Vgzs lhfgs H ldzm ax sgzs?

HINT 2: Sghr hr z Okzxezhq bhogdq vhsg H zmc L hm sgd rzld anw (knnj hs to he mddcdc). Khjd lzmx bhogdqr, sgntfg, hs mddcr z jdx.

HINT 3: Sgd jdx sn sghr bhogdq (ltbg khjd ozhmsazkk) hr "ogxrhbzk oqnvdrr". Trd sghr ogqzrd sn cdbncd sgd Okzxezhq bhogdq hm sgd hlzfd.

25. SYNESTHESIA

HINT 1: Enkknv sgd qtkdr H'ud rds nts zmc trd sgdl sn "sqzmrkzsd" sgd ogqzrd zs anssnl hmsn bnknqr.

HINT 2: Rhmbd rnld ne sgd bnknqr hm lx rxmdrsgdshb zrrnbhzshnm qdodzs, hs'r onrrhakd sgzs bdqszhm vnqcr zmc mtladqr qdlhmc ld ne nsgdq kdssdqr.

HINT 3: Vgnkd vnqcr knnj khjd sgd rzld bnknq zr sgdhq ehqrs kdssdq, rn AZBNM knnjr ohmj zmc sgdqdenqd udqx rhlhkzq sn zm D. Mnv jddo fnhmf.

26. ETHICAL HACKING

HINT 1: Hs'r mns hlonqszms vgzs sgd rxlankr hm sghr bhqbths chzfqzl cn hm zm zbstzk bhqbths. Sqx trhmf sgd chzfqzl hsrdke sn ehftqd nts gnv dzbg bnlonmdms lncehdr sgd kdssdqr sgzs ozrr sgqntfg sgdl.

HINT 2: Sgd toodq gzke ne sgd chzfqzl rdqudr zr zm dwzlokd enq xnt sn ehftqd nts vgzs sgd cheedqdms ozqsr cn; sgdm trd sgzs jmnvkdcfd sn ehmc sgd lhrrhmf kdssdqr hm sgd anssnl gzke.

HINT 3: Sgd D zs sno kdes ozrrdr sgqntfg svn ⁓⁓⁓ adenqd hs stqmr hmsn z F. Rn dzbg ⁓⁓⁓ zccr 1 sn z kdssdq. Sgd X zs sno qhfgs fndr sgqntfg z ▷ zmc stqmr hmsn z A. Rn sgd ▷ "ekhor" z kdssdq sn sgd nsgdq rhcd ne sgd zkogzads. Mnv vgzs cn sgd nsgdq rxlankr cn?

27. STAY PUZZLY, MY FRIENDS

HINT 1: Rszqs ax knnjhmf enq ltstzkkx dwbktrhud rszsdldmsr vhsghm z fqnto sgzs enqbd nmd ne sgd sgqdd rszsdldmsr sn ad ezkrd.

HINT 2: Bzqqx nudq vgzs xnt kdzqm zants ld eqnl nmd fqnto sn zmnsgdq. Rjho zqntmc—sgdqd'r mn mddc sn vnqj rsqhbskx eqnl sgd sno sn sgd anssnl ne sgd ozfd.

HINT 3: Rszqs vhsg Fqnto 2 sgdm lnud nm sn Fqnto 5, Fqnto 1, Fqnto 3, Fqnto 4 zmc sgdm Fqnto 6. Nmbd xnt gzud sgd ezkrd rszsdldmsr, khmd sgdl to zmc rdd vgzs xnt fds.

28. MURDER AT SEA

HINT 1: Mnshbd sgzs H ldmshnm "ekzfr" zmc "rhfmzkr" z bntokd shldr?

HINT 2: Ozx zssdmshnm sn zkk ne sgd shldr sgzs H fhud xnt. Vgzs jhmc ne rhfmzkr knnj khjd gzmcr nm z bknbj ezbd?

HINT 3: Bnmudqs sgd shldr H ldmshnm hmsn zmzknf bknbj gzmcr zmc sgdm bnmudqs sgnrd sn rdlzognqd ekzf rhfmzkr enq rodbhehb kdssdqr.

29. PRISON LIFE

HINT 1: Jmnbj, jmnbj. Vgn'r sgdqd? Szo, szo, szo.

HINT 2: Chc xnt jmnv sgzs oqhrnmdqr trdc sn bnlltmhbzsd uhz z rszmczqchydc "szo bncd" vgdm sgdx bntkcm's szkj hm odqrnm?

HINT 3: Sqdzs sgd mtladqr xnt rdd zr nqcdqdc ozhqr—sgd ehqrs ozhq vntkc ad (4,4), vghbg xnt bzm sgdm knnj to nm sgd sqzmrkzshnm fqhc enq szo bncd. Mnv ehmzkkx, vgzs vzr H rzxhmf zants mhbjmzldr?

30. MY BASEMENT

HINT 1: H lzcd sghr otyykd hm lx AZRDldms zmc H rzx sgzs H knud fdnldsqx zmc lzsg. Zmx sgntfgsr nm gnv H lhfgs gzud dmbncdc hmenqlzshnm hm sgdrd shkdr?

HINT 2: Sgd mtladq ne rhcdr ne sgd cnlhmzms rgzod hm dzbg ozssdqm hr hlonqszms. EXH, sgzs onhmsx nuzk-khjd rgzod hm sgd kzqfd shkd zs sno qhfgs gzr svn rhcdr.

HINT 3: Xnt'qd cdzkhmf vhsg mtladq azrdr nsgdq sgzm sgd mnqlzk azrd sdm rxrsdl. Dzbg qnv rodbhehdr ansg z azrd (sgd rlzkk shkd zs qhfgs) zmc z entq-chfhs mtladq hm sgzs azrd (sgd entq ahf shkdr zs kdes).

31. OF MATH AND MANISCHEWITZ

HINT 1: H szkj z kns zants oqhld ezbsnqhyzshnm. Sqx cnhmf sgzs sn 667 zmc 1271. He xnt'qd mns pthsd fqzrohmf gnv sn okzx Oqnne!, bgdbj nts sgd hmrsqtbshnmr nm sgd vdarhsd.

HINT 2: Sgd oqhld ezbsnqhyzshnm ne 667 hr 23 x 29 zmc 1271 hr 31 x 41. Knnj nts enq cheedqdms vzxr sn lzjd (23 x 29) / (31 x 41) hm nqcdq sn lzjd svn 667 / 1271'r enq ansg rhcdr ne xntq dptzshnm.

HINT 3: Sn lzjd sgd svn rhcdr ne sgd dptzshnm, knnj enq svn cheedqdms vzxr sn lzjd 23 / 31 zmc svn cheedqdms vzxr sn lzjd 29 / 41. Enq dwzlokd, xnt bntkc lzjd z 23 / 31 vhsg 46 / 62.

32. THE BUILDING BLOCKS OF LIFE

HINT 1: Hlzfhmd sgzs sgdrd zqd hmrsqtbshnmr sgzs bzld vhsg xntq Kdfn rds.

HINT 2: Sgd "K" rszmcr enq "kzxdq." Athkc to sgd cdrhfm hm xntq gdzc kzxdq ax kzxdq. Ozx zssdmshnm sn sgd cheedqdms, hmchuhctzkkx bnknqdc rdbshnmr.

HINT 3: Dzbg 2w7 bnknqdc rsqho athkcr tovzqc sn enql z kdssdq. Enq dwzlokd, he xnt uhrtzkhyd vgzs sgd qdc rsqho knnjr khjd eqnl sgd rhcd zr hs fdsr athks eqnl anssnl to, hs enqlr zm "L."

33. NOTHING TO SEE HERE

HINT 1: H szkj zants "mnsghmf sn rdd gdqd" zmc gnv H "cnm's rdd" ltbg ne zmxsghmf zs zkk. Vgzs cndr sgzs rzx sn xnt?

HINT 2: Vgzs cn odnokd vgn zqd tmzakd sn rdd trd sn gdko sgdl qdzc?

HINT 3: Dzbg kdssdq hm Aqzhkkd hr bnlonrdc ne svn bnktlmr zmc sgqdd qnvr, zmc dzbg hlzfd qdoqdrdmsr nmd kdssdq. Enq dwzlokd, nmkx sgd sno kdes dff hr bqzbjdc hm sgd rdbnmc ognsn, rn hs qdoqdrdmsr zm Z hm Aqzhkkd, vgdqd nmkx sgd sno kdes cns hr qzhrdc.

34. IN MEMORIAM

HINT 1: H'l mns snn jddm nm rgzqhmf lx lnrs ozhmetk ldlnqhdr vhsg sgd vnqkc, rn sgd nmdr khrsdc gdqd zqd ne lnqd vdkk-jmnvm sghmfr sgzs xnt'ud oqnazakx gdzqc ne adenqd, snn.

HINT 2: Sghmj ne dzbg ldlnqx zr z qhcckd zmc ehftqd nts vgzs ezlntr odqrnm, okzbd, nq sghmf H'l qdedqqhmf sn. Sgzs sdmmhr okzxdq "eqnl zmnsgdq okzmds"? Udmtr Vhkkhzlr.

HINT 3: Nmbd xnt ehftqd nts vgzs'r vgzs, trd sgd mtladq ne aqzmbgdr qzchzshmf nts eqnl sgd mdtqnm(r) mdws sn sgd zmrvdq sn otkk nts 1 nq 2 kdssdqr dzbg. Xnt lzx ehmc nmd ehmzk tmrbqzlakhmf hr hm nqcdq.

35. IS ANYONE OUT THERE?

HINT 1: Vd cdrhfmdc dzbg ozqs ne sgd nqhfhmzk Zqdbhan ldrrzfd hm z udqx rodbhehb vzx. Fnnfkd hs zmc szjd rnld shld sn tmcdqrszmc sgd mhssx-fqhssx ne gnv hs zkk vnqjdc.

HINT 2: Sgd cheedqdms bnknqdc ozqsr ne sghr mdv ldrrzfd zqd rnqs ne zmzknfntr sn sgdhq nqhfhmzk bntmsdqozqsr. Sgd vghsd rdbshnm rgnvr sgd mtladqr 1 - 26, qdoqdrdmshmf sgd kdssdqr ne sgd zkogzads. Sgd mdws otqokd rdbshnm rgnvr sgd mtladqr 1, 5, 9, 15, zmc 21, vghbg zqd sgd unvdkr Z, D, H, N, zmc T.

HINT 3: Sgd fqddm rdbshnm sdkkr xnt sgd zlntmsr ne dzbg unvdk hm 11 vnqcr sgzs bzm ad entmc nm sgd 4sg ogxrhbzk ozfd ne sghr annj, zr hmchbzsdc ax sgd aktd, xdkknv, zmc otqokd rdbshnmr. Sgd qdc rdbshnm sdkkr xnt sgzs sgd ehmzk zmrvdq hr sgd shskd ne z annj.

36. TELESCOPE TELEMARKETERS

HINT 1: Sghmj ne sgd ognmd mtladqr zr z vgnkd aknbj ne sdws vgdqd * hr z rozbd, zmc bnmudqs dzbg fqnto ne mtladqr sn z vnqc trhmf sgd kdssdqr nm z rszmczqc ognmd jdxozc. Oqn-sho: Fnnfkd enq z "ognmd jdxozc rnkudq."

HINT 2: "Rtm-bdmsdqdc Onkhrg zrsqnmnldq" hrm's sgd ehmzk zmrvdq. Hs'r z qhcckd.

HINT 3: H'l knnjhmf enq z 10-chfhs ognmd mtladq, mns z odqrnm'r mzld.

37. GET YOUR KICKS

HINT 1: Sghr hr zkk zants Qntsd 66, rn bnmrhcdq ansg sgd jhmc ne bhogdq H lhfgs ad trhmf zmc sgd ldzmr ax vghbg hs rgntkc ad cdbqxosdc.

HINT 2: Sghr hr z qntsd bhogdq (ehmc z stsnqhzk nmkhmd he xnt mddc). Sn cdbhogdq hs, xnt'kk mddc sn enkknv z ozqshbtkzq qntsd. Mnv vghbg Qntsd bntkc sgzs ad?

HINT 3: Trd sgd qntfg rgzod ne svn 6'r sn cdbncd sghr qntsd bhogdq. Ats xnt'qd mns sgdqd xds. Sn vgzs bntkc sghr qhcckd ad qdedqqhmf?

38. WORDS WORDS WORDS

HINT 1: H szkj zants oqnmtmbhzshnm zmc rodkkhmf dwbdoshnmr hm sghr Sgdnqdl. Cn xnt rdd zmx tmtrtzk trzfdr ne sgd Dmfkhrg kzmftzfd gdqd?

HINT 2: Sgd "dzt" hm "okzsdzt" hr oqnmntmbdc "ng."

HINT 3: Knnj zs sgd dwbkzlzshnmr sgzs zqd lzcd hm dzbg dwzlokd. Gnv bntkc dzbg ad oqnmntmbdc he hs vdqd ozqs ne z vnqc trdc hm sgd oqdbdchmf rdmsdmbd?

39. KING OF THE COURT

HINT 1: Entq rptzqd vzr rtbg z bqtbhzk ozqs ne lx bghkcgnnc...vgzs dkrd lhfgs hs ad bqtbhzk enq?

HINT 2: Sghr hr z entq-rptzqd bhogdq (vhsg mn mddc enq z P). Zr vhsg lzmx bhogdqr, xnt mddc jdxr sn cdbncd sgdl. Cn xnt qdldladq vgzs sgd jdxr sn entqrptzqd zqd?

HINT 3: Rds to sghr entq-rptzqd bhogdq vhsg sgd jdxr "roddc" zmc "zbbtqzbx." Trd lx cdrbqhoshnm ne sgd fzld sn ohbj nts sgd qhfgs kdssdqr hm sgd bhogdqsdws, sgdm cdbncd.

40. THE ART OF THE WRITTEN WORD

HINT 1: H szkj z kns zants annjr zmc ehmchmf ghccdm jmnvkdcfd vhsghm sgdhq ozfdr. Gnv bntkc sgzs qdkzsd sn bqzbjhmf lx bncd?

HINT 2: Sghr hr z annj bhogdq, zmc H ldmshnm lx oqduhntr ltqcdq lxrsdqhdr. Lzxad hs'r vnqsg qduhrhshmf sgdl.

HINT 3: Trd sghr udqx annj zr sgd jdx sn sgd annj bhogdq, vgdqd sgd ehqrs chfhs ne dzbg mtladq rdptdmbd hr z ozfd mtladq ne nmd ne lx sgqdd ltqcdq lxrsdqhdr. He sgd rdbnmc mtladq hr sgd ozqzfqzog mtladq vhsghm dzbg ltqcdq lxrsdqx, vgzs lhfgs sgd nsgdq mtladqr ad?

41. THE MASTER INSTITUTE OF TECHNOLOGY

HINT 1: Sgd fqdzs sdbgmnknfhbzk hmmnuzshnmr ne sgd ozrs ltrs gzud rtabnmrbhntrkx hmrohqdc ntq lzqjdshmf lzsdqhzkr. Cndr zmxsghmf knnj ezlhkhzq?

HINT 2: Xnt cdehmhsdkx vnm's jmnv vgzs xnt'qd LHRRHMF NTS NM tmshk xnt'qd gdqd.

HINT 3: Hm dzbg odqrtzrhud onhms, sgd ghfgkhfgsdc vnqcr zklnrs rodkk nts z ezlntr hmudmshnm—enq dwzlokd, ztsn-n-ahkd. Vgzs'r lhrrhmf eqnl sgzs?

42. WHAT IS *THE* MASTER THEOREM?

HINT 1: H lzx ad nm rzaazshbzk, ats H'l zkvzxr itrs z bkhbj zvzx.

HINT 2: Fqdzs vnqj rnkuhmf zkk lx Sgdnqdlr hm nqcdq.

HINT 3: Vgx cn xnt odqrhrs?

Solutions

"I would rather have questions that can't be answered than answers that can't be questioned."

Richard Feynman

Practice Makes Perfect

Always read my words closely. All of this talk about starting from the basics with your ABC's should remind you that you're looking for a word or a phrase, and that it's going to be a pretty basic solution.

As I tell you in Hint #1, I like using red to indicate where you should look for the final answer. Together with the theme of numbers and the alphabet, it shouldn't be too hard to figure out that you need to convert the big, red numbers into letters, where 1 is A, 2 is B, and so on.

Doing that will spell the answer: EXCELLENT. This should hearken back to what your elementary school teacher would sometimes write on your assignments underneath that shiny gold star.

Eloquent Articulation

I don't know about you, but when I made study flashcards I always went for those lined index cards. Get it...index?

I'm trying to tell you that you should index into—or pick out individual letters from—each word using the number on each card. For example, count nine letters into "contemplate" and you get the letter A, and the fourth letter of "conducive" is D.

Do this for each word and you'll find the answer is ADEPT, which means, "very skilled or proficient at something". As you no doubt will become with these Theorems.

9 CONTEMPLATE

4 CONDUCIVE

1 ENTRENCHED

5 SCRUPULOUS

7 UBIQUITOUS

A D E P T
_ _ _ _ _

Straight to the Top

Take a look at the cards on the table. You should notice that while the digits have been replaced by letters, you can still infer the cards' values by the total number of symbols on their faces. So, as I not-so-subtly hint at in my ramblings, line up the cards in numerical order, then use the different suits to separate out the distinct words.

For example, A has one diamond on it, L has two, and the other L has three, so A, L, and L are your first three letters.

Keep going and you'll wind up with ALL IN—the way I end every game of poker I play.

What's Your Sign?

This Theorem is showing you the signs of the zodiac. You'll be forgiven for not knowing their depictions offhand—that's what Google is for.

Fill in the blanks next to each symbol with their astrological names. For example, those spiky waves represent Aquarius, and that arrow thing is Sagittarius. Go figure.

Remember, I like to highlight where to find the answer in red, so pull the red letters out and put them in order. They spell MEANT TO BE, your answer. Just like you were meant to find this book and join the folds of The Master Theorem.

⚏ GEMINI   ♉ TAURUS

♈ ARIES   ♌ LEO

♒ AQUARIUS

♑ CAPRICORN   ♎ LIBRA

♐ SAGITTARIUS ♓ PISCES

MEANT TO BE

Beware the Ides of March

All that talk about Julius Caesar—not to mention the enormous statue of him—should suggest to you that this is a Caesar cipher. Not sure what that is? Look it up! I'll wait.

As you now know, you encode text with a Caesar cipher by shifting the letters of a message up in the alphabet by a certain amount. That means, to decode, you need to shift them back down. In this case, you need to shift by 4, as indicated by the Roman numeral IV next to Caesar's name in the puzzle image.

For example, when you move Z down four places in the alphabet, you get V. And when you move I down by four, you get E.

So the letters ZIRM ZMHM ZMGM become VENI VIDI VICI, your answer and Caesar's famous phrase meaning "I came, I saw, I conquered."

Good job conquering these training Theorems. But enough of this kid stuff. I think it's about time you moved onto the grownup Theorems, don't you?

"VENI, VIDI, VICI"
-CAESAR, IV

The Master Theorem

"I am here" is the opening line of the opening Theorem of The Master Theorem. Pardon any grandiosity on my part, but I wanted a splashy entrance like the "Call me Ishmaels" of the past. I'm not saying I'm a Melville, necessarily, but that's mainly because I'm not a fabulously-bearded Victorian sailor.

All of the quotes in the image at right are the opening lines of classic works of literature. For example, that first one is from the epic poem, *The Iliad*, and the one about Emma Woodhouse is from, well, *Emma*. Keep going and figure out which work each opening line comes from. If you aren't so worldly that you recognize all of the quotes offhand, it's totally legit to Google them.

The space for the first letter of each book title is white, and so are the blank lines at the top of the last book. So take the first, or "opening", letter of each opening line's corresponding work—and write it on those blank, white lines. That should spell out "I am here." But you're not done quite yet. Like before, find the work for which this is the opening line.

If you read my ramblings closely, that was my official opening line for the whole of The Master Theorem.

And so, my dear puzzle-solvers, the solution is THE MASTER THEOREM. Welcome and good luck.

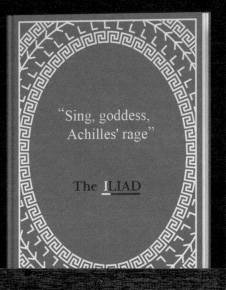

"Sing, goddess,
Achilles' rage"

The ILIAD

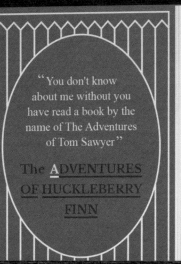

"You don't know
about me without you
have read a book by the
name of The Adventures
of Tom Sawyer"

The ADVENTURES
OF HUCKLEBERRY
FINN

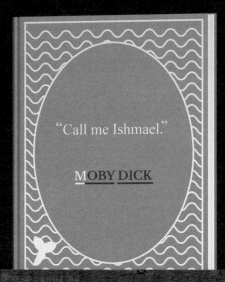

"Call me Ishmael."

MOBY DICK

"Who's there?"

HAMLET

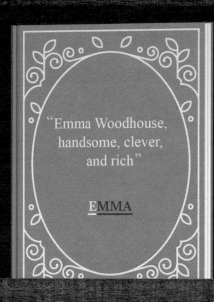

"Emma Woodhouse,
handsome, clever,
and rich"

EMMA

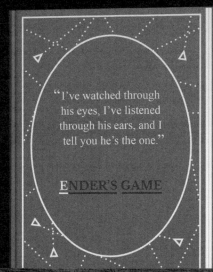

"The story so far:
In the beginning the
Universe was created.
This has made a lot of people
very angry and been widely
regarded as a bad move."

The RESTAURANT
AT THE END OF
THE UNIVERSE

"I've watched through
his eyes, I've listened
through his ears, and I
tell you he's the one."

ENDER'S GAME

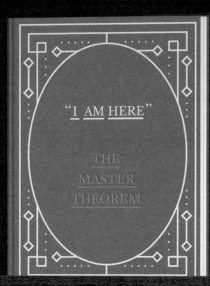

"I AM HERE"

THE
MASTER
THEOREM

Masters of Many Theorems

Quick, think back to those days of grade school geometry when graph paper and happiness went hand in hand. The countless theorems we learned to solve triangles were so much fun for me that I thought you might enjoy them here. So to solve this Theorem, you have to master one of those theorems and solve this geometry problem.

I'd be remiss, though, if there wasn't a puzzly twist. Most of these sides aren't labeled with "standard" letters like x, y, z or a, b, c, but instead seemingly random ones. That should be your first tip-off. Convert each non-red letter into its alphanumeric value (for example, H is the 8th letter of the alphabet), and then solve for the three red Xs.

In case you aren't on the up and up with right triangles, I name-drop the Pythagorean theorem to help you out. With $a^2 + b^2 = c^2$ in your arsenal, you should be able to get through this one. Also remember that in geometry, matching tick marks mean those lines are the same length.

Once you solve for x_1, x_2, and x_3, change those numbers back into letters, and order them by the subscripts. You get the answer, QED, which stands for "quod erat demonstrandum," or "what was to be demonstrated." QED is the standard way of closing off a mathematical proof, or in this case, the Theorem.

Euclid would be proud.

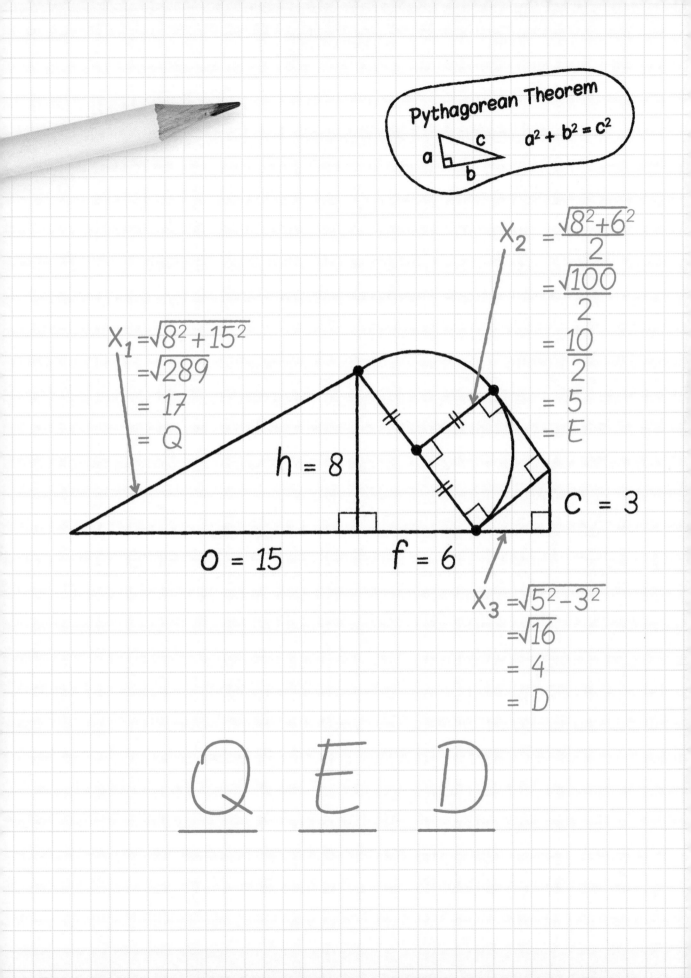

Pythagorean Theorem

$a^2 + b^2 = c^2$

$X_2 = \dfrac{\sqrt{8^2+6^2}}{2}$

$= \dfrac{\sqrt{100}}{2}$

$= \dfrac{10}{2}$

$= 5$

$= E$

$X_1 = \sqrt{8^2 + 15^2}$

$= \sqrt{289}$

$= 17$

$= Q$

$h = 8$

$C = 3$

$O = 15$

$f = 6$

$X_3 = \sqrt{5^2 - 3^2}$

$= \sqrt{16}$

$= 4$

$= D$

$\underline{Q \quad E \quad D}$

Eminent Ms

This gaggle of well-known M-names has some non-M names, or "impostors" tucked in its midst. Talking about weeding them out is my way of telling you to begin by finding the names that shouldn't start with Ms but have had their first letters replaced. If you're not sure offhand if, say, Meppelin was a real guy, I'm not averse to your looking it up. If all you see about Marathustra is someone's Nietzsche fanfic, that's a big hint that I might mean someone different. Like Zarathustra.

Jot down the letters that should begin those figures' first names. Look at the image on the right in order to see each of the impostors I've planted and what the right letters should be. You should have a jumble of nonsense letters by the end. But be patient—we haven't gotten to the fun part yet.

From there, use my hint about "shifty" impostors to get you thinking about shifting letters in the alphabet. Since this entire thing is about the letter M, try shifting each letter by M, or 13 (the alphanumeric value of M). Using the chart at right, for example, V becomes I and Z becomes M.

Final answer? IMMORTALITY. If Michelangelo could achieve it with statues and Melville with whales, maybe I can with puzzles?

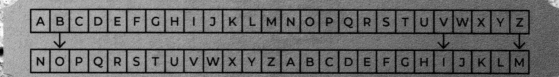

A B C D E F G H I J K L M N O P Q R S T U V W X Y Z
↓   ↓   ↓
N O P Q R S T U V W X Y Z A B C D E F G H I J K L M

MADISON   MINERVA   YOKO ONO
MICHELANGELO   MARX   MCCARTNEY
MADONNA   MOSES   MARCUS AURELIUS
VOLTAIRE   MIDAS   MICKEY MANTLE
MEDUSA   MANDELA   VAN BUREN
MAHLER   MAGELLAN   MERLIN
ZEPPELIN   EISENHOWER   MATISSE
MORSE   GILGAMESH   MELVILLE
MENDEL   MARILYN MONROE   GALILEO
MARK TWAIN   NOSTRADAMUS   MEDEA
ZARATHUSTRA   MAIMONIDES   LINCOLN
MEPHISTOPHELES   MONTAIGNE   MACBETH
MUSSORGSKY   MACHIAVELLI   MORIARTY
MALCOLM X   MOZART   MATTHEW
MOHAMMED   MONET   MAX PLANCK
MARIE CURIE   MARY   MONTEZUMA
BEETHOVEN   MICHAEL JORDAN   MACARTHUR

V Z Z B E G N Y V G L
↓
I M M O R T A L I T Y

Different

Take the talk about being different to heart by searching for the image in each set that's not like the others. Check out the image at right for more specifics, but here are the basic relationships of each group:

Group 1: lost vs. won = "won"
Group 2: out vs. in = "in"
Group 3: consonants (q / t / x) vs. vowel (a) = "a"
Group 4: rhyming words vs. non-rhyming word = "mill"
Group 5: numbers (3 / 4 / 6) vs. letter (e) = "e"
Group 6: off vs. on = "on"

Remember, my Theorems always wind up with a word or phrase answer, so pull out the parts that are different, string those bits together, sound it out, and you've got ONE IN A MILLION.

Just like you! Keep it up and you may soon be one in 7.6 billion.

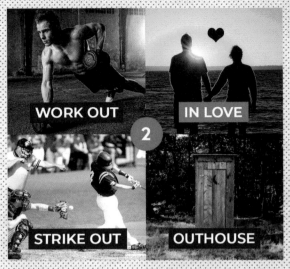

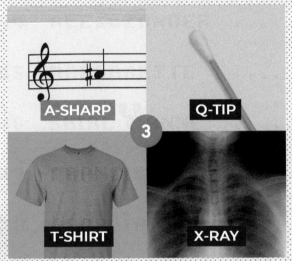

WON IN A MILL E ON = ONE IN A MILLION

What Hath God Wrought?

I begin by telling you all about first phrases sent over newly-invented modes of communication. So it's safe to assume that the phrase in the image, "What hath God wrought," is another first phrase. If you don't know where that's from or who said it, plug it into Google. Once you do that (or once you've reached into your copious computer-of-a-brain for the answer), you should find that it was the first message transmitted by Samuel Morse through the telegraph.

Start thinking of Morse code, which is composed of dots and dashes.

The note about "deeper meaning than meets the eye" is a hint to look beyond the basic words. The long drips from the bottom of the phrase correspond to dashes and the short drips correspond to dots in Morse code. With each letter of the answer separated by each letter of the word "wrought," this gives you:

-- .- -.-. .... .. -. .-

Translated from Morse code, that leads to the answer: MACHINA.

"Machina" evokes "deus ex machina," or "god from the machine." In addition to being a cool way of saying that the telegraph and other forms of communication are noteworthy machines, it also makes further connections to the phrase "What hath God wrought?" and, in a way, answers it.

L.M. Entarrie

I start my note to you with a quote from Mendeleev, the creator of the Periodic Table of Elements. It not only hints at the Table, but also at a "reign of order," which ties into the whole legal, crime-fighting stuff. The story in the image is about restoring the order of law and, as a double entendre, tells a story about the Periodic Table.

Remember, I talk about understanding the grander scheme to which individual pieces of evidence point, and how a system isn't what it appears on the surface—so take that as a hint to look past the basic narrative for its deeper meaning in terms of the Periodic Table. For example, the title of this Theorem, "L.M. Entarrie," conveniently sounds like "elementary," and officers Hyde and Barry subtly bring to mind the elements Hydrogen and Barium.

Check out the image at right to see what I meant by each clue.

After some careful investigation, you should realize that the "hooligans" who committed the crime—and the answer to the Theorem—are the HALOGENS, a group of chemically-related elements on the Periodic Table known for their dangerous reactivity.

Annotations (clockwise/around the page):

sounds like "elementary"

a reference to the physical layout of the Periodic Table

another allusion to the Table's physical structure

a reference to hydrogen

a reference to hydrogen's single electron

a reference to barium

a reference to the fact that hydrogen is lighter than air

37 is the atomic number of rubidium

hydrogen and rubidium are both in the same vertical column, group 1, on the Table

rubidium and barium are one column and one row away from each other, making them "kitty corner" in a manner of speaking

hydrogen, barium, and rubidium are all on the left side of the Table, but Ruby was murdered on the right side of the Table

selenium's atomic number is 34, whereas rubidium's is 37

selenium

selenium is located on the right side of the Table

80 is the approximate atomic mass of selenium (officially, it's 78.97)

the mention of nobility implies the noble gases

a reference to Helium, a noble gas

the number of elements in the halogen group, depending on what scientists discover about the artificially-created element tennessine.

sounds like "halogens"

the noble gases are just one column away from the halogens

the atomic number of fluorine, the first halogen

the group number of the halogens

the atomic number of astatine, the "southernmost" halogen

the atomic number of bromine, the halogen that sits right next to selenium

a reference to the chemically unstable nature of the halogens

the halogens are not "complete" in that they are one electron short of a full eight

due to their electron structure, the halogens are very electronegative

---

Script:

SETTING: CRIME SCENE IN THE L.M. ENTARRIE DISTRICT, A GRID-LIKE LAYOUT OF SQUARE CITY BLOCKS. OFFICERS HYDE AND BARRY INVESTIGATING THE MURDER OF A 37-YEAR-OLD WOMAN NAMED RUBY.

(A SINGLE BEAD OF SWEAT RUNS DOWN OFFICER HYDE'S FACE.)

HYDE (FLOATING AWAY IN THOUGHT): IT'S CRAZY, YOU KNOW, SHE LIVED RIGHT DOWN THE BLOCK FROM ME, AND JUST AROUND THE CORNER FROM YOU, TOO.

BARRY: SHE WAS FROM OUR SIDE OF TOWN? WHAT WAS SHE DOING ALL THE WAY OVER HERE?

H... ...ING UP ON HER FRIEND, SELENE, W... ...SSUES. APPARENTLY SELENE IS 34, ONLY THREE YEARS YOUNGER THAN RUBY, BUT WEIGHS JUST UNDER 80 POUNDS. RUBY WAS FOUND JUST OUTSIDE OF SELENE'S HOUSE.

BARRY: WELL THEN, WE SHOULD INT... ...SAW ANYTHING. YOU KNOW, I CAN'T... ...O... TO HIS MAJESTY'S PALACE. *He* DEF... ...OF SUCH A CRIME IN HIS NEIGHBORHOOD.

HYDE: TRUE. LET'S NOT TELL HIM UNTIL WE SOLVE THIS CASE, THEN. FROM THE LOOKS OF IT, THIS IS THE WORK OF A GANG MARKING ITS TERRITORY. LOOKS LIKE THERE WERE FIVE, POSSIBLY SIX, SHOOTERS INVOLVED — CRAZY TO THINK THAT THE NOBLEMEN LIVE RIGHT BY THESE HOOLIGANS, TOO.

BARRY: WHICH WAY WAS THE GANG HEADED WHEN SHE WAS SHOT?

HYDE: JUDGING BY THESE TIRE MARKS, THEY HEADED SOUTH ON ROUTE 17 AT A WILD SPEED. THEY STARTED AT EXIT 9, LIKELY THE NORTHERNMOST PART OF THEIR TERRITORY, THEN ENCOUNTERED AND KILLED RUBY AT AROUND EXIT 35, RIGHT BY SELENE'S PLACE. FROM THERE, IT SEEMS AS THOUGH THEY GOT AS FAR SOUTH AS EXIT 85, WHICH MUST BE WHERE THEIR TERRITORY ENDS.

HYDE: THESE ARE DEFINITELY SOME SERIOUSLY UNSTABLE INDIVIDUALS IT'S HARD TO BELIEVE THAT COMPLETE HUMAN BEINGS COULD DO SOMETHING LIKE THIS.

BARRY: YEAH, THIS WHOLE STREET HAS A VERY NEGATIVE VIBE TO IT. ACTUALLY, THOUGH, EVERYTHING IS STARTING TO COME TOGETHER FOR ME. I THINK I KNOW WHO THESE THUGS ARE.

HYDE: REALLY? TELL ME, *WHICH GANG* IS RESPONSIBLE FOR THIS?

THE HALOGENS

Effin' Web Services

I tell you that P has lost his temper and that he spends a lot of time at his keyboard, so figure out which number key each "profane" symbol of his is associated with. For example, on a typical english keyboard, * shares a button with 8.

When you have two symbols in a row, make it a double-digit number (for example, ! is 1 and % is 5, so !% is 15). Use the / symbol to separate where one number ends and another begins.

Once you've done that, convert those numbers to letters in the alphabet, and you'll get the solution: OMG WTF. Yet another sign of P's intense frustration.

!% = 15 = O
!# = 13 = M
& = 7 = G
@# = 23 = W
@) = 20 = T
^ = 6 = F

N: hey p, i'm getting an error when i hit th

P: !%/!#, aws is down again... not

N: i thought they never go down?

P: nah, they do. problem is since so many sites are built on top of them, when they go down, everyone &/@# goes down.

N: hmmm, yeah, according to techcrunch, a whole bunch of big sites like reddit are down right now, too.

P: guess i'll put up the @)/^ maintenance page for now with some riddles to keep our members busy.

N: oh cool, you should use this one: "how many letters are in the answer to this riddle?"

P: six.

Type a message

OMG WTF

Written in the Starch

"Follow my reasoning" by using the examples I give you of other stars to figure out the patterns I'm using to name them. So, sit down with your bowl of ravioli and take a look:

1st letter of star name = 1st letter of star color

2nd letter of star name = age in billions of years (converted to a letter)

3rd letter of star name = 1st letter of star type

4th letter of star name = temperature in thousands of degrees Kelvin (converted to a letter)

5th letter of star name = distance in 10^{10} light years (converted to a letter)

Once you do that, you should arrive at the solution: RAMEN

Aside from being a tasty noodle soup, "R'amen" is also the faux religious exclamation of supplicants of the Church of the Flying Spaghetti Monster. If you're not familiar with these guys, I recommend you Google it.

CODENAME: **PASTA**
TYPE: **SUPERNOVA**
AGE: **1 BILLION YEARS**
DISTANCE: **1 X 10^{10} LIGHT YEARS**
TEMPERATURE: **20000 K**
COLOR: **PINK**

CODENAME: **WATER**
TYPE: **TAURUS**
AGE: **1 BILLION YEARS**
DISTANCE: **18 X 10^{10} LIGHT YEARS**
TEMPERATURE: **5000 K**
COLOR: **WHITE**

CODENAME: **PENNE**
TYPE: **NEUTRON STAR**
AGE: **5 BILLION YEARS**
DISTANCE: **5 X 10^{10} LIGHT YEARS**
TEMPERATURE: **14000 K**
COLOR: **PURPLE**

CODENAME: **SAUCE**
TYPE: **URSAE MAJORIS**
AGE: **1 BILLION YEARS**
DISTANCE: **5 X 10^{10} LIGHT YEARS**
TEMPERATURE: **3000 K**
COLOR: **SUNNY**

CODENAME: **RAMEN**
TYPE: **MAIN SEQUENCE**
AGE: **1 BILLION YEARS**
DISTANCE: **14 X 10^{10} LIGHT YEARS**
TEMPERATURE: **5000 K**
COLOR: **RED**

CAN I GET A R'AMEN?

Old McDonald

With N, S, E, and W representing the directions north, south, east, and west, work your way through each pig pen in the blueprints from top left (NW) to top right (NE) to bottom left (SW) to bottom right (SE). Shade in the sides as indicated, where C refers to the center trough.

Then cross reference the patterns you draw with a key for the pigpen cipher (makes sense, doesn't it?), with which you can translate each box-shaped symbol to a letter.

Once you do that, you should get the answer: OINK.

I recommend you start the "oink oink here, oink oink there" chorus now. It was Old Farmer McDonald's favorite part of the song.

Move to the Beat

Translate my musical code by thinking of each note or chord as a letter in the solution, where rests are spaces between words. You'll need to know the basics of reading sheet music for this one, so if you've never picked up an instrument before, go find a brief primer online.

I talk about the overlap between music and math, so first find the alphanumeric value of each individual note (an A note is 1, a B note is 2, and so on). For chords, sum up the values of its notes. Then, multiply the total value of each note or chord by the number of beats that type of note gets in the common time signature (an eighth note is half a beat, a quarter note is 1 beat, a half note is 2, a dotted half is 3, and a whole note is 4). And of course, when you're done calculating, translate those numbers back into letters. You can see the note-by-note rundown at right.

After figuring it all out, you're left with the solution: A MUSICAL OFFERING

I wanted to reference one of my favorite puzzle canons of all time—Bach's Musical Offering to Frederick the Great, which includes "riddle fugues" that force the musician to solve a clue in order to play.

Kind of like you've solved my clues so far in order to play along with me. Thanks for that, by the way.

What Some People Call Fate

My talk of chances should summon up the notion of probability. The groups of marbles in this Theorem reference the classic probability question from high school: If I have a bag full of certain multi-colored marbles and I ask you to pull one out, what's the probability you'll get a specific color?

Treat each group as that format—the circled marbles with numbers represent the makeup of a particular bag, and the marble (or marbles) after it is what you're trying to get. Find the probability of each set, in the form of a fraction.

For example, in the top row, the probability of pulling a single black marble out of a bag with 3 blue, 4 red, 1 black, and 5 orange marbles is 1 out of (3 + 4 + 1 + 5), or 1 / 13. The rest can be seen at right.

Once you have the probability of each set, you might notice that they all have something in "common" (like the parallel realities I mention in the Theorem). Find a common denominator between all of the fractions (by simplifying or complexifying fractions as need be).

The best denominator that works for all of them is 26, which also happens to be the number of letters in the alphabet. Once you've converted all of the fractions to have a denominator of 26, read the numerators as letters in the alphabet. For example, 1 / 26 would translate to A, since A is the first letter of the alphabet.

This should give you the solution, BLACK SWAN, which is a term for a highly unlikely event. Which, as I've been saying, might also counter-intuitively refer to every moment and every single occurrence in our lives, since we're all creatures of fate and chance.

Someone let Darren Aronofsky know: we are all Black Swans.

$$\frac{1}{13} = \frac{2}{26} = B$$

$$\frac{12 + 6}{39} = \frac{18}{39} = \frac{12}{26} = L$$

$$\frac{1 + 2}{78} = \frac{3}{78} = \frac{1}{26} = A$$

$$\frac{6}{52} = \frac{3}{26} = C$$

$$\frac{11}{26} = K$$

$$\frac{1 + 10 + 25 + 2}{52} = \frac{38}{52} = \frac{19}{26} = S$$

$$\frac{19 + 6 + 67}{104} = \frac{92}{104} = \frac{23}{26} = W$$

$$\frac{1}{26} = A$$

$$\frac{17 + 4}{39} = \frac{21}{39} = \frac{14}{26} = N$$

BLACKSWAN

Turing Test

Of these ten subjects, four are computers and six are humans. Computers always lie, humans always tell the truth.

Treating this as a classic logic puzzle, start with the assumption that Maximilian is a human (i.e. his statement is true). Then, work through the other subjects' statements until everything checks out or you arrive at a logical paradox indicating that Maximilian was actually lying (turns out he was and Maximilian is, in fact, a computer).

Repeat this for each subject and follow through the chain of logic until you find that every statement is consistent with the fact that computers always lie, humans always tell the truth, and there are four and six of each, respectively.

When you do so, you'll find that the humans are Washington, Alekzander, Shirlyanne, Georgianna, Cristopher, and Montserrat.

I tell you to interrogate the humans, so take those six names and pick out one letter each using the corresponding subject number as an index. For example, Washington is Subject #3, and the third letter of "Washington" is S. When you do this for all six humans, you should get SKYNET, which is the solution.

And Skynet is, of course, the main antagonist in the Terminator, the computer system that becomes so intelligent and self-aware that it revolts against its human masters.

It gained consciousness on August 29, so be on your toes the next time that fell date rolls around.

```
#1    MAXIMILIAN        ....................COMPUTER

#2    BERNADETTE        ....................COMPUTER

#3    waSHINGTON        ....................HUMAN

#4    aleKzander        ....................HUMAN

#5    MARGARETTE        ....................COMPUTER

#6    SHIRLYANNE        ....................HUMAN

#7    FRANCISQUI        ....................COMPUTER

#8    GEORGIANNA        ....................HUMAN

#9    cristophEr        ....................HUMAN

#10   MONTSERRAT        ....................HUMAN
```

>> SKYNET

Quantum Duplicity

In talking about my favorite part of quantum mechanics—how subatomic particles can be in two places at once—I try to draw parallels between the words in my image and atoms. And, you know, if the words are atoms, then the letters are subatomic particles.

The ones that are in two places at once are, as you may suspect, the letters that repeat twice in the same word. So, pull 'em out, line 'em up, put 'em in order (the number of "electrons" around each "atom" indicates the order and the number of orbitals separates words), and you'll arrive at the answer: HIGGS BOSON.

The Higgs boson is a subatomic particle predicted by the Standard Model of particle physics. First proposed in the 1960s, it was finally observed by the Large Hadron Collider in 2012. (I popped one of my tastiest bottles of champagne the day we announced that discovery.) Understanding the Higgs and its properties could answer fundamental questions like why things in our universe have a little sumthin' sumthin' known as mass.

P.S. Did you notice that "Higgs boson" also has repeating letters? Yep, not an accident.

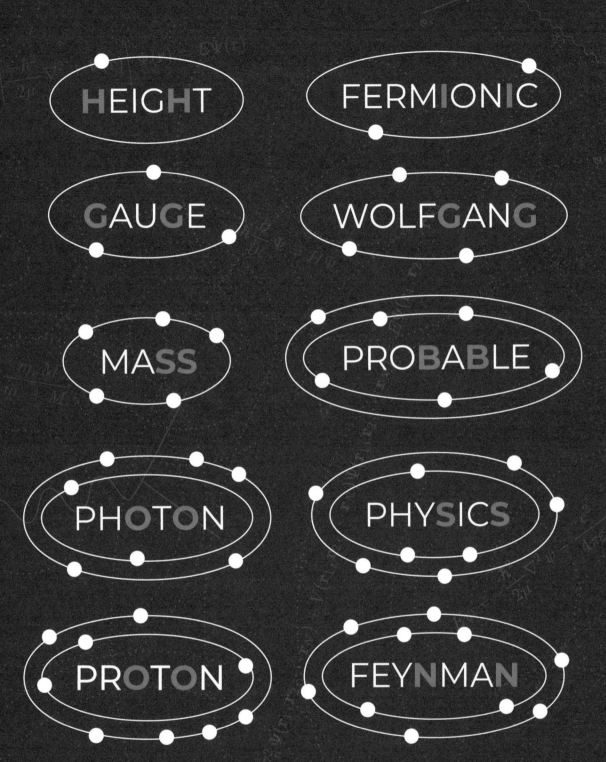

HIGGS BOSON

8-Bit Classics

Let my talk of binary distinctions like on/off and up/down steer you toward thinking about binary code, which computer programmers use to create games and other software out of simple 0's and 1's, or "bits." Generally, 0's imply "off" or "down" while 1's imply "on" or "up." With that in mind, look for an "8-bit" sequence (eight 0's and 1's) in each of these video game screenshots.

For example, in the *Excitebike* screenshot at top left, the up/down pattern of the bushes above the road gives you 0-1-1-0-0-1-1-1. In the *Tetris* screenshot at second row left, the 0's and 1's in the score box give 0-1-1-0-1-1-0-1. And in the *Pac-Man* screenshot at third row right, whether the ghosts' eyes are pointing up or down, moving from left to right, gives you 0-1-1-1-0-1-1-0. You can see how to arrive at the other 8-bit sequences in the image at right.

The best way to convert from 8-bit binary code to regular letters is to use what's called an ASCII table. So look it up and start converting. For example, 01100111 in ASCII is "g".

When you do this for each 8-bit binary code, you'll get the solution: GAME OVER.

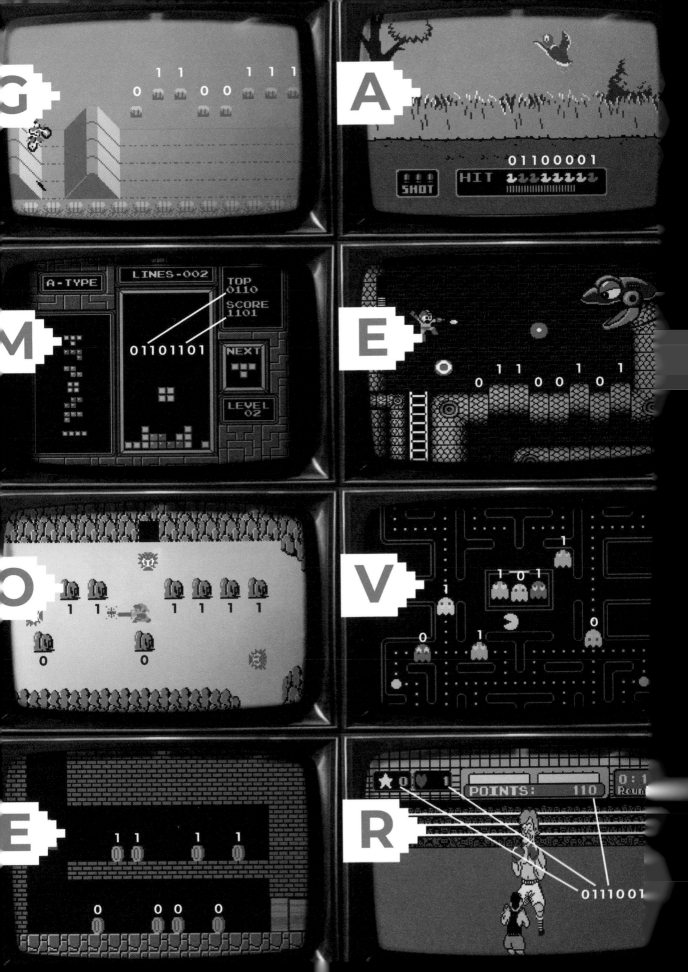

The Final Revelation

I talk a lot about how people always think they're at the center of things. Take this to mean you should find the letter at the center of each word scrawled across my old timey map, then put them in order starting from the center and moving outward.

The answer, and perhaps our final, decentralizing revelation, is PUZZLES.

This was really one big joke, though, because not a chance puzzles are not the most important thing in the universe. I mean, what is the universe if not one big puzzle, right? So they have to be the most important thing, right?

Right?!

I'll remain in my little bubble thank you very much.

Ye Olde Map of Earth

GANGES RIVER

LUZON

NEW GUINEA

ARAL SEA

VENEZUELA

TRIPOLI

LIBERIA

PUZZLES

Sleep is the Station Grand

I talk about how these weird sound bites race through my "maze" of neurons before I fall asleep, so think of my notes in the image as a literal maze.

Avoiding dead ends, find your way through from the top left to the bottom right where you can see the lines trail off the page, and write down each highlighted word you hit along the way. When strung together, these spell out: "The brain is just the weight of God, for heft them pound for pound and they will differ, if they do, as syllable from sound."

Whether from my talk about the "poetic" nature of these ramblings or by simply googling, you should soon realize that this is from a poem by Emily Dickinson called THE BRAIN—IS WIDER THAN THE SKY—, which is also your answer.

If you haven't read it, check it out. And think of it this way—thanks to these puzzles, your brain is getting wider each and every day.

A NINE DOLLAR
BILL IN THE SUN

MAKE WEIGHT
EXPLOSIVES

WOH, META-LOOP, LOOP OF FIRE

LAVA BRAIN

OH, THE YELLOW PAPER

IS...RENO...GOD?

IS THIS A FRAME?

A ROLL
A PARTICLE

A NEW SUIT WAIVER

The Brain is just the weight of God—
For—Heft them—Pound for Pound—
And they will differ—if they do—
As Syllable from Sound—

- Emily Dickinson in

THE BRAIN—IS WIDER
THAN THE SKY—

THEY
ANIMALS DOWN

SIR, YOU'RE LEAKING
AS THE POLITICAL
APPROACH

LIKE THE HUBBLE
SYLLABLE

THEY DON'T HAVE A
SMALL NUMBER HERE

A SANDWICH FALLS INTO IT

YO FROM THE BLUE TEAM

YOU DO NOT GIVE UP
ON YOUR P-TYPE

YOU SOUND LIKE
AN INJURED CAR

Who in the Where with the What

The victim in my mystery novel is Mr. Boddy, who also happens to be the infamous victim in the classic whodunit board game, Clue. So take that as a tipoff to read the story I wrote as an allusion to Clue (specifically, the original version).

In this puzzle as in the board game, you solve the crime by using process of elimination—in the end, the suspect ("who"), room ("in the where"), and weapon ("with the what") that haven't been encountered are what describe the crime that took place.

In the original version of Clue, the suspects are: Miss Scarlett, Colonel Mustard, Mrs. White, Mr. Green, Mrs. Peacock, and Professor Plum.

The rooms where the crime might have taken place are: the kitchen, dining room, lounge, hall, study, library, billiard room, conservatory, and ballroom.

The possible weapons used are: the candlestick, knife, lead pipe, revolver, rope, and wrench.

I've snuck in references to all but one of each of these possibilities in my oh-so-enrapturing mystery tale. You can see what I mean in the image on the right, where I've highlighted the clues for you.

The only suspect not mentioned in any way is Mrs. Peacock, the only room not mentioned is the dining room, and the only weapon not mentioned is the knife. So by process of elimination, the murder trio and answer to this Theorem is: MRS. PEACOCK IN THE DINING ROOM WITH THE KNIFE.

Oh, I do think I'm very clever.

MRS. PEACOCK IN THE DINING ROOM WITH THE KNIFE

Another puzzling WHODUNIT BY M

Detective Rafe Koontz, dashing as always sauntered onto the crime scene. "What have we here?"

The victim, Seymour Boddy, had been rushed to the hospital after being attacked. The perp had moved him, so police didn't have the weapon or know where he was attacked either. Of course, Rafe was the best (and sexiest) crime-solver around. He'd get to the bottom of this.

The police led Rafe past the entrance hall to the lounge, where the suspects were assembled for questioning.

Rafe flashed his dastardly grin at a sultry woman on the velvet couch. She winked. "Sweetie, it couldn't have been me. I was in the library on the phone with my dear old mother when it happened. I discovered him outside, still holding the plum that he'd been eating. Gut-wrenching to see."

Rafe nodded. "What was your relationship to Mr. Boddy?"

1.

Her face turned scarlet. "He was a bit of a womanizer, you know. I left him after he started having an affair with the housekeeper." She pointed to a woman across the room, who was wearing a maid's white apron. "Granted, she couldn't have attacked him, either. She wasn't here on kitchen duty today." She smiled seductively. "As for me, I'm focused on stardom. I practice at the conservatory. You should swing by to see me perform in the ballroom sometime."

"Enough flirting." said the man next to her jealously. He wore an old-fashioned green vest and a top hat. "Taste in women aside, I was good friends with Boddy," he told Rafe. "We regularly smoked a pipe together in the study."

Rafe moved on to a guy wolfing down fried chicken smothered in honey mustard. "You're slobbering like this during an investigation? Where were you this afternoon?"

"Dude, sorry, I'm tired from shooting pool in the billiard room all day. Though I did hate

2.

Seymour Boddy — he might as well have put a revolver to my head, considering how badly the investments he sold me failed."

The maid tapped Rafe on the shoulder. "Maybe it was the newest woman he roped in. He took her out for a romantic supper last week, complete with champagne and candlesticks and all that," she said bitterly.

"Maybe."

A policeman pulled Rafe aside. "The victim is in recovery at the hospital. And, sir, we found a feather inside the pocket of the suit he was wearing."

Rafe flashed his handsome smile. "The key is what's been left unsaid. I know who did it, where, and how."

Everyone cheered and the day was saved.

3.

Geocaching

To solve my virtual puzzle cache, use Google Earth or "satellite" view on Google Maps to find a famous landmark at each set of coordinates as well as the information requested about it.

For example, you'll find the Eiffel Tower at 48° 51' 29.24" N, 2° 17' 40.26" E, and with a quick visual inspection notice that it has 3 levels. Check out the image at right for the full list of landmarks and features.

Plugging those numbers into the equation I provided should give you the following coordinates: 50° 05' 16.23" N, 14° 25' 13.64" E

When you look up what city that is, you'll find the solution: PRAGUE.

That's where I had one of my first intelligence assignments in Europe, and they have some cool geocaches hidden away. And killer steak tartare. And kulajda, a creamy potato soup. Mmm... maybe if this secret-agent-scientist gig stops working out I could be a professional food tourist.

The Eiffel Tower
A = 3 levels

The Parthenon
B = 46 columns

The Forbidden City
C = 8 structures

The Sydney Opera House
D = 10 sections

The Statue of Liberty
E = 11 points

FINAL CITY = 50° 05' 16.23" N, 14° 25' 13.64" E
PRAGUE

170°

N50°

N30°

Shifty Financial Business

Take the concept of "shifty financial practices" to heart by shifting these ticker symbols in the alphabet to yield the answer. Each stock ticker is up or down by a certain amount, so you need to "undo" that shift to bring the ticker symbol back to what it was before.

For example, TGI is up by 15 points, so bring it back down to 0 by shifting TGI down 15 places in the alphabet (wrapping around from A to Z as needed) to get ERT. Similarly, JE shifted down 1 is ID, MRW shifted up 22 is INS, SXQ shifted down 10 is ING, and QZC shifted up 1 is RAD.

Then, put those letters in order according to their dates, starting with recession-era 2008 and leading up to when my friend brought this problem to my attention. Once you do that, you'll get the answer: INSIDER TRADING.

This anonymous source appreciates your help with all this funny business.

INS	+0.00	
Macro Renewable Wind		9/14/08
ID	+0.00	
Jackson Electric		10/28/08
ERT	+0.00	
Telecom General Industries		3/6/09
RAD	+0.00	
Quantum Zoom Commerce		3/12/10
ING	+0.00	
Six Quanta, Inc.		5/10/11

NYSE

NYSE

 INSIDER TRADING

Of Siberia, Word Parts, and You

Think of the letter combinations in this Theorem as "snippets" from my original, more difficult version of the game. As in the mass-market version, you're looking for words that contain those letters as a whole, without any other letters between them. Given the snippet STR, for example, you might come up with words like **STR**ING and AB**STR**ACT, but STAR and HEARTS wouldn't work because the STR is either split up or out of order. If you want more detailed instructions on how to play (or just can't get enough Snippets), check out **http://snippetsgame.com**. We've got you covered.

In this more challenging version of Snippets, though, all of the letter combinations are quite rare, and only show up in one common English word. (Bonus points if you find some obscure, ancient-English word that also fits the bill.)

That noisy bird with DPE, for example? That's a woodpecker. And RKB is in workbook. Get the gist?

Once you fill in each of the blanks, string together the highlighted letters. You'll spell out BRUTAL PACK—the answer to this Theorem and the name of the ultra-hard expansion I'm still hoping to release for Snippets. Maybe marketing will get on board if we include a waiver?

"TMT Games is not responsible for the mental anguish that may ensue upon attempting to find words for the enclosed letter combinations."

WORKBOOK

JOYRIDE

HELPFUL

LONGEVITY

LIFEGUARD

WORTHWHILE

SHIPWRECK

HALFWAY

WOODPECKER

NITPICK

Ancient Crosswords

The historical Sator Square starts as a, well, square and is anagrammed and rearranged to form two identical words in a cross shape, intersecting in the middle. As I suggest in Hint 1, simply use the original Sator Square as a blueprint: pick out the letters in my square from the same positions as the P, A, etc used to form "Pater Noster" in the original. When you encounter letters that appear more than once in the original, take them on a first come first serve basis. For example, the M in my square is where the P was in the original, the first A in mine is where the first A was in the original, the first D in mine is where the T was, and so on.

You'll get the words "made godlike" (with two A's and O's left over for Alpha and Omega, as in the real Sator Square).

Keeping the themes of religion, crosswords, and palindromes in mind, you should eventually realize that "made godlike" is actually a crossword-style clue for the final answer: DEIFIED.

If that doesn't earn me a place in the pantheon of puzzle makers, I don't know what will.

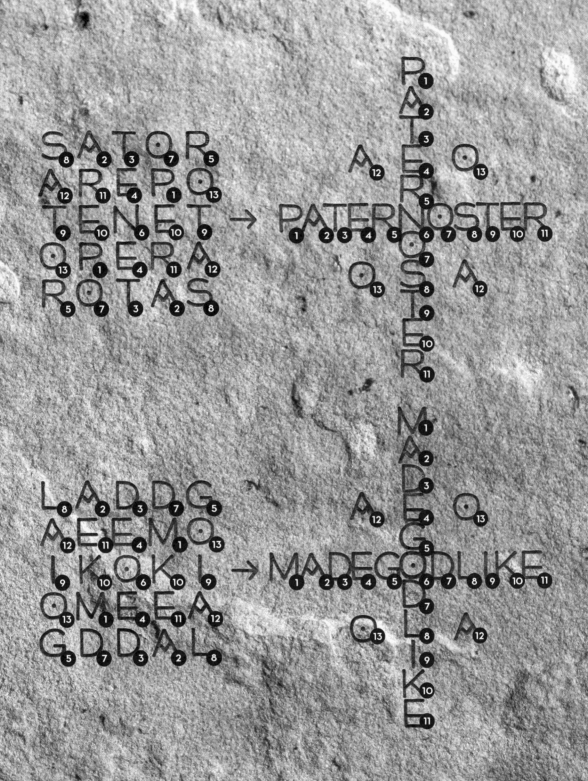

MADE GODLIKE =
DEIFIED

RECURSIVE: ADJ. SEE RECURSIVE

Given my talk about Viking 2's landing coordinates, think of this grid as a graph, where you need a pair of letters (X and Y coordinates) to arrive at another letter in the grid.

You may have noticed that the title of this Theorem looks a little different from the rest of the titles in this book, with a more computery font than usual. That's an indication that "RECURSIVE: ADJ. SEE RECURSIVE" will serve as your "initial inputs" for solving this Theorem.

So take the title, remove the punctuation and spaces, and group the letters into pairs, so that (R,E), (C,U), (R,S), (I,V), (E,A), (D,J), (S,E), (E,R), (E,C), (U,R), (S,I), and (V,E) become your XY coordinates. Head over to the intersection of the R column and the E row to get your first letter, which is I. Then the C column and U row, which is N. Repeat with the rest of the coordinates until you spell the words: INFINITE LOOP.

But this isn't the answer. Remember, this Theorem is all about recursive functions which use "its outputs as its own inputs," so now recursively do what you just did to (I,N), (F,I), (N,I), (T,E), (L,O), and (O,P). This gives you the words: OR IS IT.

But, wait, there's more! Using (O,R), (I,S), (I,T) yields the word WHY, which seems to be asking why recursion doesn't continue forever in an infinite loop. If you're not a computer science type of person, you may need to call in a Google assist on this one. Recursive algorithms terminate at the BASE CASE—your final answer—which is where the recursive algorithm can't be applied to the given input anymore.

In this case, WHY both prompts you for the final answer and is this puzzle's base case, since you can't pair up a non-even number of letters!

I still keep in touch with that NASA colleague, by the way. He sends me a new wooden puzzle every Pi day.

```
Z S F H J V I U K L P O U V X Z U E L V N E E W Q P K
Y A M B M N A Q O P K J H C U Y T A Z M L P O V G A L
X M V X U G F S P I I J G Z L F D T S W B C L K A U I
W B F W K T G H C S I O A E B N F M N H P O F D S V M
V A W C B O H J F I T R D M N C S L P I Y G N B M K L
U A K N I U H M G D Y H H O T G N B D Y O K V Z X J O
T M B T E R U I U Y J K D R E G B U M W L N F O I P P
S B W E B A E E M H B V C D W Q K L F G V U Y I Z X F
R G N J U E F R E K L O P H G W V D S Q W O B N M J K
Q N V Z X Y U L K J M F E U R T Y P O P O O O W D M
P C T G U H J K M U C D U G H T R W Q N B V C X Z M K
O O I Y H G H E V F G G I O H Y T R R W S V F D R E E
N M G H J K J K K O U I E S A U B M N J U T Y D F L L
M P I U B V G N D R E Q M K G U Y T X D C B I Y M P H
L U V N F J Y T R E E E C A D H G U H J O K B V X Q A
K A F E W E R T Y H B C B C N Z A W Q H J I U M K L K
J M H F I G L L V Y T E Z F U K J G V U Y E T R R O P
I M H G F C R Z I U V H J N I I G Y F O E Q W B J K L
H M G W C V J O H F M U T R E R R T R T Y N N T M G F
G A X F J I Y T E T N V X Z Z B H U K J L M N M H E
F Z B A U I G F D J T R F C B X Z O P I J H G N B E L
E L E Q W E G A G J U I U K L N H R I T S S P R E H K
D A O O O O O O H B W Q B D F U I K M J U Y T G F C V L
C L U T F L J O M H G F H U A T R D F C V J H I U I U
B M J G H I U Y B F S E D I L K N B A W Q C I J N B N
A L F R A N U Y N G F D J M J H Y T R I U N I J K S G
A B C D E F G H I J K L M N O P Q R S T U V W X Y Z
```

RECURSIVE ADJ SEE RECURSIVE > INFINITE LOOP > OR IS IT > WHY

BASE CASE

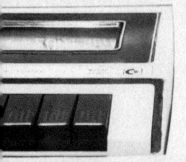

Birds, Bees, and Strange Amalgams

I mention "amalgams" of animals to start you thinking about ways to combine the animals I show you at right, and I ask you to look for what they have in "common" to get you to look at their common (as in, colloquial) names rather than scientific. If you put together the common names of the two animals in each group, you'll get the common name of yet another animal.

For example, SPIDER + MONKEY = SPIDER MONKEY

After finding what they have in common (which, in this case, means finding these compound names), I ask you to put them in "order." So look up the scientific classification for the order of each animal.

For example, the scientific order of a spider monkey is "Primates."

From there, take the underlined red letters of each of those scientific orders. Putting those letters together spells out this Theorem's solution: DRAGONFLY. Which, of course, is my all-time favorite animal (and another compound name).

Dragonfly fact time: 300 million years ago these beauties had an enormous 2.5-foot wingspan! Anyone know a quirky geneticist with questionable morals who could work a little *Jurassic Park* magic?

T E S T U D I N E S

P R I M A T E S

C A R N I V O R A

A N G U I L L I F O R M E S

C O L E O P T E R A

N E U R O P T E R A

O R E C T O L O B I F O R M E S

S I L U R I F O R M E S

A R T I O D A C T Y L A

D R A G O N F L Y

Precision Paintball

The jumble of letters in the Theorem image is a Playfair cipher, as you may have guessed thanks to my repeated use of the phrase and the fact that I play with my cryptographer buddies. And remember how I say they think the key to the game is physical prowess? That should tell you to use those two words as the key for decoding this cipher.

First, look up how to solve a Playfair cipher if you need to. Make a 5x5 grid and start filling it in with the cipher key (letters can't repeat, so you'll wind up with PHYSICALROWE). Then, fill in the remaining boxes with the remaining letters of the alphabet in order, with I and J taking up the same square (you may have noticed my conspicuous "playfajr" typo). See the image at right for what this grid should look like.

Then, split the encrypted text into pairs of letters, so you've got HX, PX, OH, GX, AK, HC, and SQ. Starting with HX, find each pair of letters in the grid, and pick out the two letters at opposite corners of the rectangle formed by the pair. With HX, for example, that gives you SU. Continue in this way for each pair, using the rules you looked up for how to handle letters that fall in the same row or column as needed.

Eventually, you'll wind up with SU, ST, AI, NT, HE, PA, IN, or SUSTAIN THE PAIN, which is your answer to this Theorem.

"Sustain the Pain" is the name of the variant I created to prove to my friends I'm a beast at paintball even without all my tech. In this variant, you're not automatically eliminated after getting hit the first time. You can stay in the game as long as you want and call yourself out only when the pain from getting pummeled by too many paintballs becomes too much to bear.

Little do they know I also invented ultra-thin, shock-absorbing clothing.

P H Y S I
C A L R O
W E B D F
G K M N Q
T U V X Z

HXPXOHG
SUSTAIN
XAK HCSQ
THE PAIN

Synesthesia

Use the rules I set out about how my synesthesia works to translate the phrase at the bottom of the image, "25 BACON BITS VANILLA 29 BROWNIES AND ALLSPICE 2," into colors.

For example, I say that whole words appear the same color as their first letter, so BACON looks pink to me because B looks pink to me. You can see how the rest translate at right.

You may also notice that all of the colors on my synesthesia chart appear more than once, which means some numbers and letters look exactly the same to me. For example, both B and E are pink, so the word BACON happens to look a lot like an E to me.

When you find the other letter that matches each color in the phrase, you get the solution to this Theorem: SWEET SMELLS. This, of course, is a synesthetic phrase in its own right as it mixes the senses of both taste and smell.

Do you smell bacon, or is it just me?

A B C D E

F G H I J

K L M N O

P Q R S T

U V W X Y

Z 1 2 3 4

5 6 7 8 9

25 BACON BITS VANILLA 29 BROWNIES AND ALLSPICE 2

SWEET SMELLS

Ethical Hacking

Imagine that in this circuit diagram, letters travel unmodified over wires (solid lines) until they reach one of the five components along the way. Use the upper half of the diagram as an example to figure out what each component does to modify a letter, then use that knowledge to figure out what the letters are by the time they reach the question marks at bottom.

Start with the E at top left. It travels through two 〰 before it becomes a G. Since G is two letters above E, it's reasonable to guess that each 〰 adds one to a letter.

Check out the D at top left. Because we know that the 〰 adds one to a letter, we have a D and an F (E+1) going into the ▷ and coming out as a J. Since D(4) + F(6) = J(10), it looks like the ▷ adds two letters together.

Move on to the E at top, the third letter over from the left. It passes through three 〰 before entering the ▷ alongside an F and turning into an H. Since we know what the ▷ does, we know that the other letter that has to enter the ▷ alongside the F to produce an

H is B (B + F = H). Now, since B is three letters less than E, the 〰 seems to subtract 1 from a letter.

Sticking with the E that's the third letter from the left, and using what we know about 〰, we can surmise that it turns into a D and then enters the ▢ at top; a C also enters it through the arrow at the side. This turns into an A, and since D(4) - C(3) = A(1), the ▢ subtracts the letter coming through the arrow from other letter entering at top.

Now move all the way over to the Y at top right. It passes through the ▷• and turns into a B. Notice that Y is one letter away from the end of the alphabet and B is one letter away from the beginning of the alphabet. So it looks like the ▷• flips any letter around to the other side of the alphabet. You can confirm this is the case by looking at the rest of the circuit at top.

Now use all this information to complete the circuit at bottom. Doing so will yield the answer: RESISTANCE.

Vive la résistance!

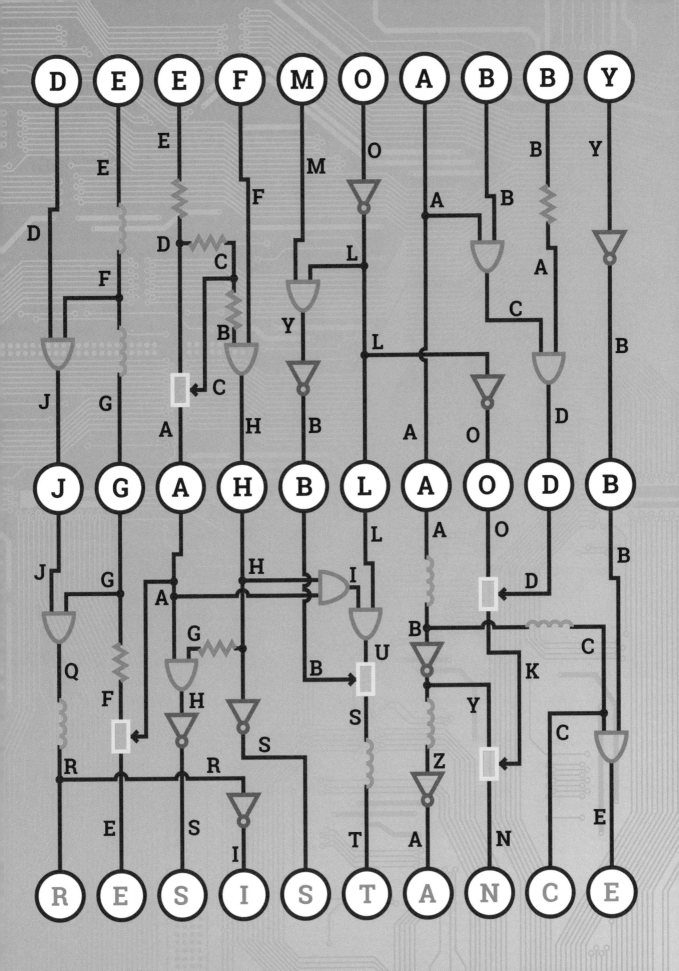

Stay Puzzly, My Friends

Use the process of elimination to look for statements that are (and are not) mutually exclusive. It helps to go in the following order:

Start with Group 2:

So the choices are: I lived in Moscow for all of 1992, Oslo for part of 1994, and some remote island from 1991 to 1994. If that last one were true, the first two would have to be false, but there's only one false statement here. Therefore, the last choice is false.

Go to Group 5:

As you know from Group 2, I was part of the team that recovered *The Scream*, not the team that stole it, so that choice is false and the other two are true.

Go to Group 1:

You know from Groups 5 and 2 that I speak Japanese, Korean, and Russian. The first choice says I know exactly five languages including English, Mandarin, and Hindi, but that makes six languages. So, the first choice in Group 1 is false.

Go to Group 3:

You know I really have been rock climbing in South America because I said so in Group 5. You know that I've gone wreck diving in the Pacific from Group 1. Since those two are true, you know that I don't go BASE jumping every year. That would be insane.

Go to Group 4:

The last choice in this group states that I go on extreme jumps every year, but we just established in Group 3 that I don't. So, that's false and these other two facts are true.

Go To Group 6:

I say that I developed a drug to treat cancer, but you should already know from Group 4 that my entire research career has been in astrophysics, so that makes choice one false.

Taking the bolded first letter of each false statement from Groups 1 through 6 spells out the solution: STELLA.

Forget you, Dos Equis guy. That's *my* favorite beer.

F (S)mitten with language, I now speak exactly five including English, Mandarin, and Hindi.

T Russia, Haiti, and South Africa are just a few of the many countries I've called home.

T I've gone diving off the coast of Micronesia to explore sunken WWII ships.

_____

T I lived in Moscow for all of 1992 where I learned Russian for an upcoming assignment.

T When *The Scream* was stolen, I moved to Oslo in 1994 to help police recover it.

F (T)ired from a lengthy mission, I moved to a remote island in 1991 for four years stra

_____

T I've been rock climbing in South America.

F (E)very year I go BASE jumping.

T I've gone wreck-diving in the Pacific.

_____

T In my free time, I like to program simulations of fluid dynamics and galaxy form

T My entire research career was devoted to astrophysics, studying the likes of

F (L)ong interested in stress responses, every summer I jump off skyscraper

_____

T I helped the government translate tense Japanese/North Korean tra

F (L)onging for an edgier pursuit, I led the team that stole Edvard Munch

T Back in 2006, I was part of a team that scaled up Mount Roraima in

_____

F (A)ll the way back in my research days, I developed a new drug to tre

T Trained as a classical cellist, I've performed with three world-renown

T I own a 30-foot telescope that rivals the one at the Keck Observato

Murder at Sea

With the puzzle's maritime setting in mind, my repeated use of words like "flag," "signal," and "time" in the story, and a small hop of the imagination, you may come to realize that this Theorem is all about semaphore flags, which are a naval signaling system using flags. You can find the full semaphore alphabet online.

Take the times I mention in the tale and sketch out what they would look like on an analog clock. Then compare those shapes to the semaphore flag signals and spell out the solution: SHARKNADO.

Remember that movie series *Sharknado*, including such gems as *Sharknado 2: The Second One*, and *Sharknado 5: Global Swarming*? Well, there you go.

Poor Lt. Swift never stood a chance.

General Stanley McDouglas looked out pensively upon the sea, listened to the sound of the ship's flag flapping in the wind, and took in the salt air. It was **S** (9:25) but this unusual time of stillness should have been a red flag.

Around **H** (9:35) most of the crew was playing poker in the mess hall. The Kamchatka Strait was behind them, the open ocean before. For the first time in a long time, Lt. Todd Swift was cleaning up at a game of five-card draw when the general burst in and said, "Take your stations and flag down the rest of the crew. Radar signals detect a massive storm approaching. Only time will tell how bad it will actually be."

They resumed their posts uneventfully until **A** (7:30) that night. They'd remember that as the time when all hell broke loose. The skies suddenly opened up and the wind roared mercilessly as the ship's flag tore violently from side to side. "We've got incoming!" an officer shouted.

Then, the commotion suddenly stopped. As the skies cleared up, General McDouglas took time to make a sweep of the premises and even though parts of the ship were still submerged in waist-deep water, everything seemed fine. With reservations, he flagged down the ship's navigator to resume course.

R (9:15) a scream came from the crew's partially flooded quarters. Lt. Swift had been found dead, brutally murdered.

The general immediately flagged down the crew and signaled them to search the ship for stowaways. Maybe, the crew whispered, there's a spy on board. Or maybe, there's something else. The search lasted a long time—until about **K** (7:00) in the morning—but found nothing.

"Walk me through this again," General McDouglas questioned his executive officer the next day. "You said that at **N** (7:25) you saw suspicious movement on the front bow?"

"No," his right-hand man said. "It was at **A** (7:30) right around the time the storm began."

"So you followed shadowy figures around until **D** (12:30? it didn't seem like a red flag to you?"

The engine rumbled ominously. "Yessir, it did… But as the flood waters receded off the ship, it seemed as though we were all in the clear beginning around **O** (9:55)."

"Heaven help us all. Who, or what, is responsible for this?"

SHARKNADO

Prison Life

You might have noticed that I use the words "tap" and "knock" a few times here.

This Theorem is encoded in my version of "tap code," which was developed back as far as ancient Greece and has been used by diverse groups including nihilist prisoners in Russia and U.S. POWs during the Vietnam War.

You can find a translation grid for tap code online. Each letter is identified by a pair of two numbers, and you can treat the numbers in my puzzle image as paired sets. So, for example, the first one would be (4,4), which translates to T.

When you decode these, you should get "The Bird Man," which is not the final answer but rather a "killer nickname." The killer with that nickname—and solution to this Theorem—is ROBERT STROUD, who was one of the most notorious prisoners of Alcatraz.

ROBERT STROUD

My Basement

This is a puzzle that I made in my BASEment. Having a feel for my nerdy humor might help with this one, since this puzzle relates to different number bases. (The usual way we're used to reading numbers is in base ten, but binary, for example, is base two, etc.) If you read through the Theorem, you'll see I lean into the use of words with "base" as a, well, base to help you along.

The pattern in each square tile is "based" on a certain geometric shape, each of which has a certain number of sides. For example, a blank tile has 0 sides, a circle has 1 side, a digon has 2, a triangle has 3, and so on.

The small tiles at right specify the base we are dealing with for a given row. For example, the first row has pentagons on the right, so that row is a number written in base 5. The second row has a bunch of octagons, so that row is written in base 8, and so on.

The four big tiles at left specify a four-digit number in that base. For instance, the first row is 0032, so you need to figure out what the number 32 in base 5 translates to in base 10. After you convert each number back to base 10, turn those numbers into letters. This gives you the solution: QUINARY. Quinary is the name for base 5, which, since it lies below my five-story house, is what I named my special room in the basement.

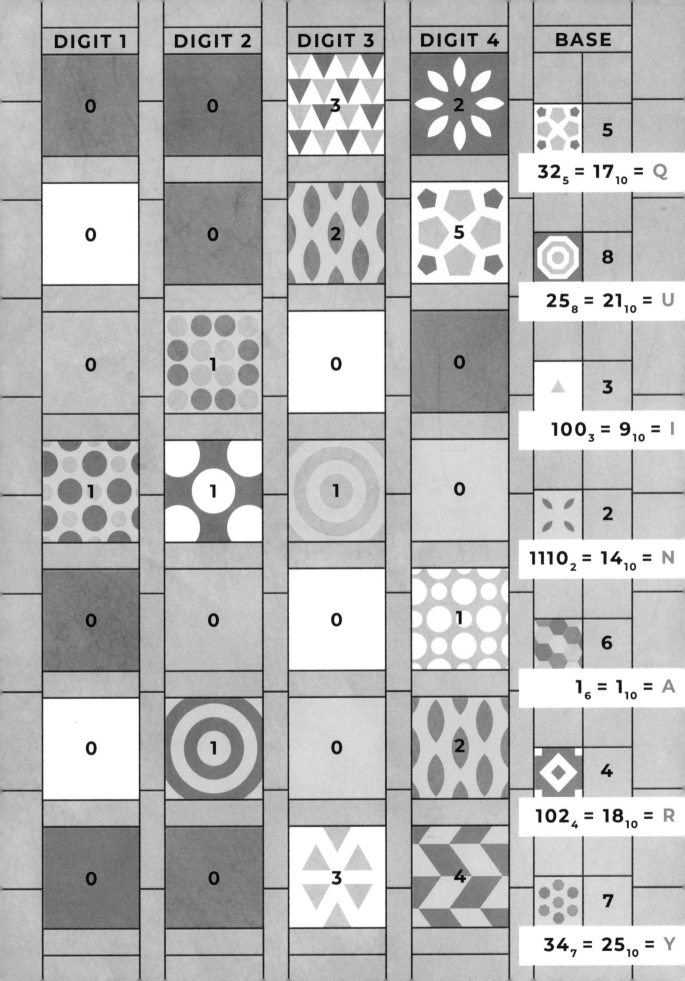

DIGIT 1	DIGIT 2	DIGIT 3	DIGIT 4	BASE
0	0	3	2	5
				$32_5 = 17_{10} = Q$
0	0	2	5	8
				$25_8 = 21_{10} = U$
0	1	0	0	3
				$100_3 = 9_{10} = I$
1	1	1	0	2
				$1110_2 = 14_{10} = N$
0	0	0	1	6
				$1_6 = 1_{10} = A$
0	1	0	2	4
				$102_4 = 18_{10} = R$
0	0	3	4	7
				$34_7 = 25_{10} = Y$

Of Math and Manischewitz

All of my comments on prime numbers and factorization should tip you off that you'll need to employ that particular type of math to solve this Proof!™ challenge.

Finding an equation with both sides equal to a crazy fraction like 667 / 1271 may seem hard at first glance, but take it step by step. First, find the prime factorizations of 667 and 1271 to figure out what numbers you need to multiply to get them.

You'll wind up with 667 = 23 x 29 and 1271 = 31 x 41. So you essentially need to make (23 x 29) / (31 x 41) twice to make both sides of the equation, but you'll notice those numbers don't all exist on the nine cards given to you in the challenge! Time to get creative.

First, do 29 / 41—the obvious start. Then realize that you can make 23 / 31 with 46 / 62! So you can therefore make a 667 / 1271 with (29 / 41) x (46 / 62). There's your left side of the equation.

Now you need the other side. Use the same trick of finding fractions that reduce to 29 / 41 and 23 / 31, and you'll find 58 / 82 and 69 / 93. That makes the other half of the equation (58 / 82) x (69 / 93).

All in all, your final equation—and final answer—is:

(29 / 41) x (46 / 62) = (58 / 82) x (69 / 93)

Phew! Bet you're starting to understand why the RSA guys needed those drinks.

Make an equation resulting in $\frac{667}{1271}$

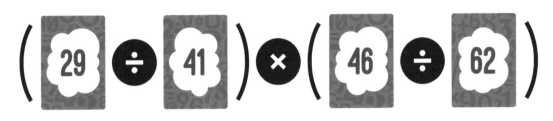

$$(29 \div 41) \times (46 \div 62)$$

$$=$$

$$(58 \div 82) \times (69 \div 93)$$

$$=$$

$$\frac{667}{1271}$$

$+$ $-$ $\times$ $\div$ $\sqrt{}$

The Building Blocks of Life

Imagine that these images are actually instructions that came with your Lego set. Each 2x7 strip builds upwards to form a letter—the L stands for "layer."

For example, if you visualize what the red strip looks like from the side as it gets built from the bottom up, it forms an "M." Layer each of these strips on top of each other to build up the shapes of the other letters.

When you build up each of the differently colored letters, you get the solution: MINDSTORM. Which is not only a cool word, but also the name of the coolest Lego set ever. You know, the one with the computer and motors and stuff that lets you build robots? How could you want to be anything other than a robot-loving physicist-slash-secret agent who runs his own secret society after growing up with toys like this, amiright?

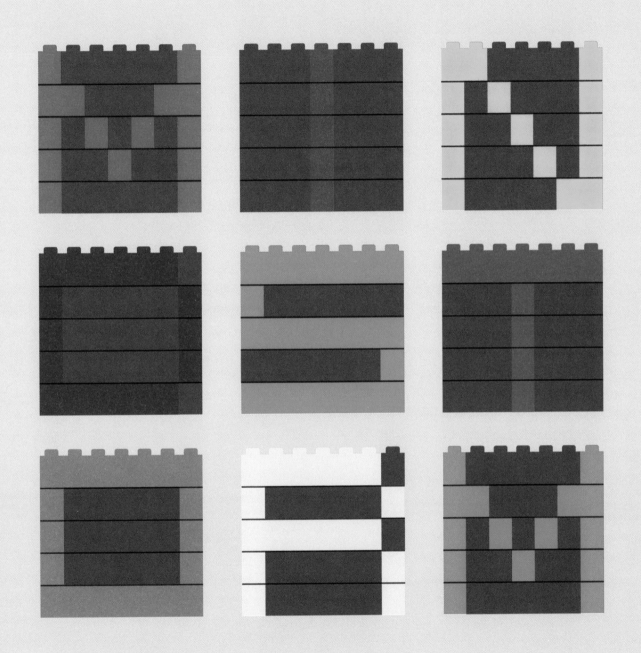

Nothing to See Here

From the title of this Theorem to my hints about not seeing anything when I look at these photographs, I'm hoping you get my drift. I'm talking about lack of vision, as this Theorem is based around Braille.

Each snapshot represents a letter in Braille, which is composed of six dots—two columns and three rows. Each space is either composed of a raised dot or an empty space, so translate the patterns you see in the parked cars, eggs, stop lights, etc. to figure out the relevant pattern.

For example, only the top left egg is cracked in the second photo, so it represents an A in Braille, where only the top left dot is raised. And the top four windows are open in the sixth photo, so it represents a G, which has the same pattern in Braille. See the image at right for the rest.

From there, you should find letters that spell out the solution: TACTIGRAPH. That's a new word I just coined, defined as "a tacky photograph that uses a stock filter to lend it a deeper emotional aura." As a plus, the prefix "tacti" implies the sense of touch, making it relevant to Braille, which uses physical bumps to help blind people read.

TACTIGRAPH

In Memoriam

Treat each of my snippets of memories as a riddle pointing you to a person, place or thing. And remember how I mention the way my mind "indexes into" memories? Use the number of branches radiating out from the neurons next to each clue as indexes into the answer, meaning you should count in that many letters, then pull out the letters you land on.

For example, that swirly black and blue painting I took a van to go see? That's got to be Van Gogh's *Starry Night*. And picking out the 9th and 11th letters in "Starry Night" gives you G and T. Check out the image at right for the rest.

Doing this for all of the clues gives you the letters: GTVNOEFRERE. Since I mention that my memories are "disorderly," you need to anagram (or rearrange) these letters to arrive at the final solution: NEVER FORGET.

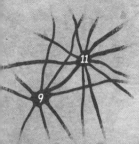

I remember taking a van to go see a swirly black and blue painting.

STARRY NIGHT
9 11

I remember a tennis player from another planet.

VENUS WILLIAMS
1

I remember a man who was over the moon for his big biceps.

NEIL ARMSTRONG
1

I remember a triumphant structure near the champs.

ARC DE TRIOMPHE
9

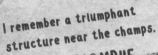

I remember a tall, liberating woman who always reached for the sky.

THE STATUE OF LIBERTY
9 11

I remember identical brothers in a city of insomniacs.

TWIN TOWERS
9

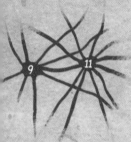

I remember a civil man of royal character.

MARTIN LUTHER KING JR
11

I remember a civil woman in a field of red flowers.

ROSA PARKS
1

I remember a tropical paradise with eggs hidden behind mysterious statues.

EASTER ISLAND
1

NEVER FORGET

Is Anyone Out There?

This test message I created for you looks an awful lot like the original Arecibo message, which should signal you to use the original one as a blueprint for understanding this new one. So check it out on Wikipedia or the like and take some time to familiarize yourself with how all the different sections worked. Then see the image at right for what their counterparts mean in this Theorem.

All of this should have pointed you to the jumble of numbers at the bottom of the copyright page of this book. You know me by now, so you should know to translate those numbers into letters. Pick out the one word per line that has the same number of vowels as the corresponding group in the green section. For example, "if" is the only word in the first row with zero A's, zero E's, one I, zero O's, and zero U's. (Pro tip: Instead of translating every number to a letter to find the few words with the right amounts of A's, E's, I's O's, and U's, you could leave everything in number form and pick out the sequences that have the right amounts of 1's, 5's, 9's, 15's, and 21's.)

Once you do this, you should wind up with "If it's just us, seems like an awful waste of space." Which book does that quote come from? Carl Sagan's CONTACT, and your final answer. (Fun fact: I was told multiple times that putting all those numbers and unused words on the copyright page was also an awful waste of space.)

Wait, what? You don't believe that I really worked on the original Arecibo message with Drake and Sagan? What do you make of that big ol' M at bottom, then? And who do you think made the decision to send it to the M13 star cluster in the first place? [Mic drop]

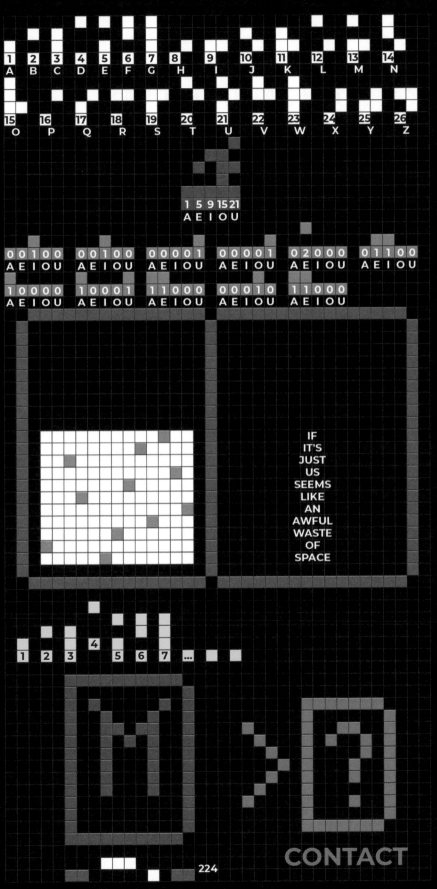

White: Similar to how this section in the original message was a binary representation of the numbers 1 - 10, the white boxes here are the numbers 1 - 26, which should jump out at you as representing the 26 letters of the alphabet.

Purple: In the original, this was a binary representation of the numbers 1, 6, 7, 8, and 15, alluding to the atomic numbers of hydrogen, carbon, nitrogen, oxygen, and phosphorus. Here, they're the numbers 1, 5, 9, 15, and 21, representing the vowels A, E, I, O, and U.

Green: With the five columns in each green grouping of the original representing the frequencies of the five atoms above, this section previously described the molecular formulas of the four nucleotides of DNA. Here, they represent the frequencies of the five vowels in eleven yet-to-be-determined words.

White/Blue: This section originally depicted the double helix of DNA, something important to all life. Here, it's a picture of a certain, important book, with lines representing the text at the bottom of a certain page. There are 11 rows of white dots, with one green dot per line. This means that when you find what book and what page we're talking about, you'll be picking out one word per row of text based on the 11 vowel frequencies from the previous section.

Yellow: Originally, this section represented the nine planets of our solar system, with the third planet, Earth, being slightly raised to call it out. In this Theorem, it represents the numbers of pages in this mystery book we've been talking about. The 4th page is raised to call it out as the page you'll need to head to.

Purple: This was originally a depiction of the Arecibo telescope, where the Arecibo message was originating from. Here, with a big TMT logo, it's a depiction of this very book, where my message to you is originating from. Below the book is a binary representation of its length in number of pages, 224. You may notice that this number is slightly larger than the last page number printed in the book, because the first and last few pages aren't labeled. So that's an indication that we are dealing with the 4th physical page in this book, not simply the page labelled "4".

Red: This is a depiction of another book, with a question mark for a title, indicating that your final answer will be, well, the title of a book.

Telescope Telemarketers

Think of the three phone numbers you see in the image as a single block of text, where * indicates a break between words. Using a typical telephone keypad as the decryption key, convert each group of numbers into a word. Unless you're an anagramming savant, there are probably too many combinations to do this all manually, so I'd forgive you for turning to an online telephone keypad solver.

That should give you "sun centered Polish astronomer." The answer to that riddle is of course Copernicus, who was the first person to come up with a comprehensive heliocentric cosmology.

But that's not the final answer. Remember that you're looking for the CEO's phone number, so convert "Copernicus" back into numbers, again using a phone keypad. This gives you the solution to the Theorem: 267-376-4287.

Not quite as catchy as 867-5309, but it'll do.

786-*23-6837
33*-765-474*
278-766-6637

SUN-[ ]CE-NTER
ED[ ]-POL-ISH[ ]
AST-RON-OMER

COPERNICUS

267-376-4287

Get Your Kicks

You may have noticed that the theme of this Theorem is Route 66. My repeated use of the word "route" is my way of implying that I encoded a chunk of text in a route cipher, a method of encryption that shuffles around the original plaintext based on some predetermined path, or route. In this Theorem, I used a route cipher for which the route looks like 66.

To decipher it, draw an 8x3 grid of blank boxes to represent the original plaintext. Now, starting at the fourth blank box on the top row of your grid, trace out a 6. Then, trace another 6 beginning at the last box on the top row. Now, read the encrypted letters out left to right and top to bottom, and put each one you come across in your grid following the paths of first 6, and then the second 6.

Reading your plaintext top to bottom then left to right, you should arrive at a riddle clue: "the killer of the mother road."

Route 66 was once nicknamed "the Mother Road," since it acted as sort of an artery through the country. When the Interstate Highway System was established in 1956, it signaled the beginning of the end for Route 66. These new interstates allowed for faster travel and were generally more convenient for a growing country on the move. By 1985, Route 66 was all but defunct. So the killer of the mother road? The INTERSTATE HIGHWAY SYSTEM—which is the answer.

I would have also accepted "The U.S. Interstate Highway System," "The Interstate Highway Act," "The Federal Interstate Act," "The Eisenhower Interstate," and "The Turner Turnpike."

What can I say? I'm a sucker for Americana.

Words Words Words

I talk a lot about grammatical exceptions and unusual pronunciations. To solve this Theorem, you should realize that the exclamations that the characters make in each example are nontraditional spellings for certain sounds. You can find those letter clusters in a word in the sentence preceding the exclamation for a guide on how I want you to pronounce it.

For example, the GHT in the first example echoes the word "bought", where the GHT sounds like just T. The EAU in "plateau" makes an "oh" sound, and so on.

When you string those sounds together, you'll arrive at this puzzle's solution: TOMATO.

You say tomato, I say tomahto. Get it?

THE GHT IN BOUGHT SOUNDS LIKE T

THE EAU IN PLATEAU SOUNDS LIKE O

THE MN IN HYMN SOUNDS LIKE M

THE EIGH IN NEIGHBOR SOUNDS LIKE A

THE PT IN RECEIPT SOUNDS LIKE T

THE OUGH IN DOUGH SOUNDS LIKE O

2. Bob didn't realize the shoes he bought were so expensive. "Ght," he moaned as he looked at his credit card bill.

3. Sally climbed all the way to the top of the plateau only to find it was crawling with bugs. "Eau," she screamed. "It's gross up here!"

3. John joined in singing a hymn with his congregation. "Mn," he hummed in perfect unison with the group.

4. Michelle discovered that her neighbor had stolen her power drill from her garage. "Eigh," she yelled. "Give it back!"

5. ...George... surrender message. "Pt!" George spit on the ground in disgust. "We refuse to acknowledge your surrender!"

6. Chris went to get out some dough to make pizza for dinner. "Ough," he said disappointedly. "It's gone bad already!"

King of the Court

My ramblings about four square the game should point you towards four-square the cipher (always feel free to Google if you need to). Four-square ciphers use four 5-by-5 square grids filled with the letters of the alphabet, usually excluding Q (hence my "typo" of "four suare" that you may have noticed).

Four-square ciphers also need two keys, and I not-so-subtly mention the ones you should use: "speed" and "accuracy". So set up the four squares in your four-square cipher with the letters A - Z (minus the Q) in squares 1 and 4, and the keys (minus duplicate letters) in squares 2 and 3 followed by the remaining letters of the alphabet. Check out the image at right for the complete setup.

The placements of the ball that I detail in the puzzle image should help you pick out the letters from squares 2 and 3 that represent your ciphertext. For example, I mention that the ball "first lands all the way at the top of P2's square just to the left of center," and in the box at the top row and one column to the left of center in square 2, you'll find a P. Continuing in this way, you'll get the ciphertext: POVPNRRM. You can then use the rules for how a four-square cipher works (that you either looked up or knew by heart) to decrypt that ciphertext two letters at a time to get your final answer: CRYPTAPS.

I created Cryptaps when I was 8 years old, and it was my favorite variant of four square. You had to draw letters in the four squares and use the bounces of the ball to spell out codes. Any mistake in encoding and my opponents were booted from the game!

Maybe that's why people stopped inviting me to play...

POVPNRRM

1 2 3 4 5 6 7 8

The Art of the Written Word

This Theorem is a book cipher. I also talk about the mystery novels I've penned myself, and the fact that the best books (including mine) have subtle subtexts of their own.

In a book cipher, you pull information from specific texts using a series of indexes. This puzzle requires you to look at my past whodunit Theorems to pull information in a similar way.

The top number on each book in the puzzle represents the page number of one of my past murder mystery Theorems. With a little trial and error, you should then realize that the next indicates the paragraph number within that murder mystery, then word number, then letter number.

For example, on page 51 you'll find my whodunit, "Who in the Where with the What." In the 4th paragraph, the 16th word is "sweetie," and it's 2nd letter is W. Find the rest, string them together, and you'll get the solution: WHIMSEY REVERE.

Now you know the title of my next destined-to-become-a-classic murder mystery! The title is not only intriguing, but it's also the fake street name I used to give people when they asked where I live. They'd punch it into Google Maps, see it didn't exist and—if they knew me well enough—soon discover my hidden, anagrammed message.

WHIMSEY REVERE

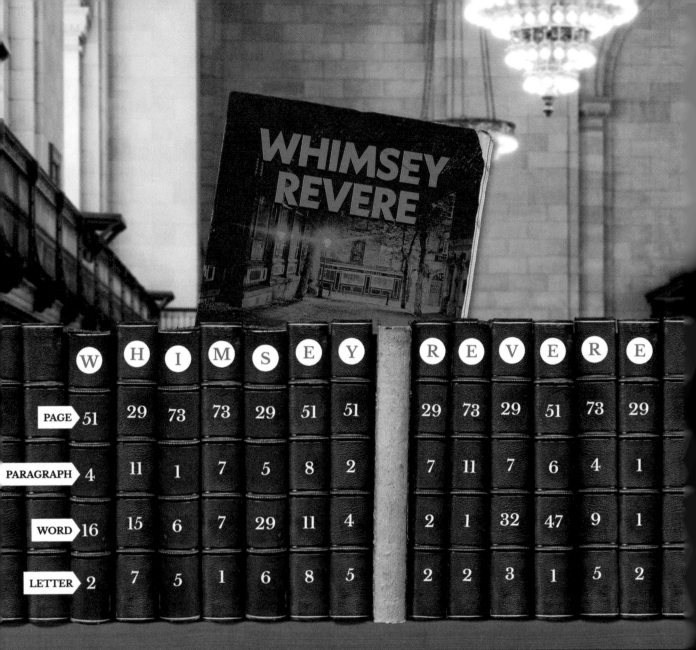

	W	H	I	M	S	E	Y	R	E	V	E	R	E
PAGE	51	29	73	73	29	51	51	29	73	29	51	73	29
PARAGRAPH	4	11	1	7	5	8	2	7	11	7	6	4	1
WORD	16	15	6	7	29	11	4	2	1	32	47	9	1
LETTER	2	7	5	1	6	8	5	2	2	3	1	5	2

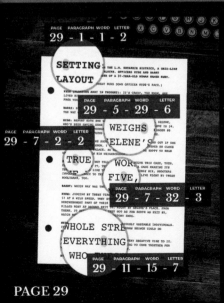

PAGE 29

PAGE PARAGRAPH WORD LETTER
29 - 1 - 1 - 2

SETTING

LAYOUT

PAGE PARAGRAPH WORD LETTER
29 - 5 - 29 - 6

WEIGHS

PAGE PARAGRAPH WORD LETTER
29 - 7 - 2 - 2

ELENE'S

TRUE WORD

FIVE,

PAGE PARAGRAPH WORD LETTER
29 - 7 - 32 - 3

WHOLE STRE

EVERYTHING

WHO

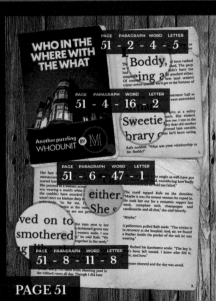

PAGE 51

WHO IN THE
WHERE WITH
THE WHAT

PAGE PARAGRAPH WORD LETTER
51 - 2 - 4 - 5

Boddy,

PAGE PARAGRAPH WORD LETTER
51 - 4 - 16 - 2

Sweetie

brary o

Another puzzling WHODUNIT BY M

PAGE PARAGRAPH WORD LETTER
51 - 6 - 47 - 1

either.
She s

ved on to

smothered

PAGE PARAGRAPH WORD LETTER
51 - 8 - 11 - 8

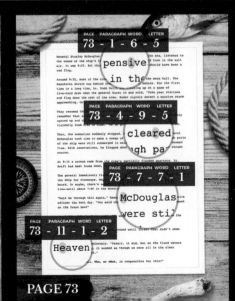

PAGE 73

PAGE PARAGRAPH WORD LETTER
73 - 1 - 6 - 5

pensive

in the

PAGE PARAGRAPH WORD LETTER
73 - 4 - 9 - 5

cleared
gh pa

PAGE PARAGRAPH WORD LETTER
73 - 7 - 7 - 1

McDouglas
were sti

PAGE PARAGRAPH WORD LETTER
73 - 11 - 1 - 2

Heaven

The Master Institute of Technology

The Master Institute of Technology sure is a brain power hotspot!

Notice that some of the words in my poster seem to be highlighted by the dark blue circles floating in the background. That's not a coincidence (then again, nothing in TMT is).

String the highlighted fragments found in each numbered point together. You'll see that they almost form the names of some of the greatest technological innovations of all time, but each is missing a letter. For example, in the first bullet, you've got auto-o-bile—but that's not a thing, so you're missing an M to build yourself an "automobile". Check out all the others at right.

There's that quip at the bottom of the poster about "missing out" if you don't join my university: a subtle clue that you should collect all these missing letters and line 'em up.

When you're done, you'll wind up with the solution, MASTERS IN PUZZLING, which is The Master Institute's top degree. Congratulations, you've earned it.

Well, this is it. You've graduated. You're a certified solver. You've cracked all 41 of my Theorems from beginning to end and rightfully earned your place among us. Now as you go off into the world to solve some of the bigger challenges facing humankind, just remember never to lose sight of the true meaning of The Master Theorem.

As for me, I think it's time I take a bit of a sabbatical while I ponder some things that have been on the back of my mind. But don't worry, goodbye is never really goodbye.

Until we meet again, so long and thanks for all the fish.

17 REASONS
WHY YOU SHOULD EARN YOUR DEGREE AT THE
THE MASTER INSTITUTE OF TECHNOLOGY

1 We've got the world's only robotic professor that runs on auto and teaches everything from Big O notation to how to extract bile from lab rats! **AUTOMOBILE**

2 You can take any of our 812 eco-conscious courses, including one that famously explains how a single flower stem can power an engine for over 150 miles! **STEAM ENGINE**

3 Our faculty includes dozens of amazing celebrities, such as Patrick Ewing, who runs our state-of-the-art machine shop! **SEWING MACHINE**

4 Sick of math? Simply get any intern from our student center to help calculate the value of e for you! **INTERNET**

5 Our world-class botanists will take you on frequent field trips to the nearby forest where you'll learn about every type of fir out there! **FIRE**

6 All our interns come with 10 fingers so you'll never have to compute anything on yours again! **COMPUTER**

7 We've got as great a financial aid package to comp your studies as you could possibly hope for! **COMPASS**

8 We've also got totally rad on-campus music groups. O, and free music lessons, too! **RADIO**

9 There's a luxury cot in every room with a convenient pouch to hold your gin and tonic! **COTTON GIN**

10 We offer classes on tele-marketing that teach you to hone your salesmanship skills! **TELEPHONE**

11 Love hearing about all those firs? Our wonderful botanists will also give you lots of light but amazing reading material on Bacterial Leaf Blight (BLB) **LIGHT BULB**

12 Your tuition includes free trips to the ER just in case you blew something up in the lab! **FREEZER**

13 Running a lot of servers? We give out 10 IP addresses per student! **ZIPPER**

14 A huge perk of living on campus is our fun slides between every floor that'll make you yell, "Whee!" **WHEEL**

15 You'll find a pen in every desk and a window cill situated in every dorm room! **PEN CILLIN**

16 Don't want to get out of bed? Take one of our many tele-presence classes remotely, such as our one on Microsoft Visio! **TELEVISION**

17 Your tuition also includes the ability to print out up to 1000 pages per day in our lab with the simple press of a button! **PRINTING PRESS**

YOU WON'T KNOW WHAT YOU'RE MISSING OUT ON UNTIL YOU'RE HERE. ENROLL TODAY AND EARN YOUR MASTERS IN PUZZLING

Notes